M000072961

DAILY H♥PE
FOR
FAMILIES

A Heartlight Devotional

DAILY H♥PE
FOR
FAMILIES

MARK GREGSTON

Forefront
BOOKS

DEDICATION

This book is dedicated to the person who I believe has had the greatest influence on my life because of the way she lives out the Scripture she loves dearly...my wife, Jan.

ACKN♡WLEDGEMENTS

When I was in the 9th grade, there was a man who has no idea of the fruit he produced in my life because of his involvement. He was the reason that I became the Oklahoma Bible Quiz Champ of 1969. His name was David Worsham. Others came who made scripture come alive in my life. Joe Mooberry, Chuck Swindoll, Doug Burr, and Chuck Madden were people I admired for their courage to share the beauty of scripture and how it can come alive in a person's life, specifically mine. You guys don't know the impact you had on me and will never know how appreciative I am of your influence on my life.

FOREW♡RD

*I*n the book of Revelation, there is a strong admonition from God to the church about not forgetting your first love, that first love meaning our leaning into, trusting, and depending on God for all our needs. And yet in the world today, there is every distraction available to keep you from remembering anything about your first love.

Mark Gregston's passion for first loving parents and teens has been witnessed for over thirty-five years. His passion for releasing this new devotional is not only to celebrate the years of experience he's had living with over 3,000 teens at the Heartlight residential counseling center he and his wife founded, but to help parents stay focused and determined to change the destiny of their family as well. The Parenting Today's Teens radio program and podcast has been effective in helping hundreds of thousands by offering hope and healing through any storm. He reminds all to remember their first love through trusting God to meet them in those storms of life that sometimes divides parents and teens.

I believe you'll find a word of encouragement and help to not only re-center your day, but to also remind you of trusting and leaning into your first love.

Michael Blanton
Blanton Entertainment
Songwriting University

INTRODUCTI♡N

The busyness of life sometimes keeps us detached from the people and things closest to our hearts. If you're like me, you get too involved in the trivia of life and are not engaged in the essentials that sustain you and invigorate you toward "love and good deeds."

My prayer for you is the same prayer the apostle Paul shared with the Ephesians, that the eyes of your *heart* may be filled with *light* so that you may know the *hope* to which God has called you. It is with this prayer in mind that I selected a Scripture for each devotional and coupled it with a few words of encouragement. I hope you'll spend some time reflecting daily on the importance of God's Word in your life and figure out how to make that become a living reality in the life of your family.

I hope these devotionals will help you turn words into actions, put legs on Scripture, express the eternal through relevant application, and take wisdom from God and share it with your family.

May God take the words from this devotional and use them in a mighty way to encourage you to be that parent or grandparent your teen children need you to be. Blessings upon you as you strive to be to your kids who God has been to you.

Mark Gregston

> *"The LORD does not look at the things people*
> *look at. People look at the outward appearance,*
> *but the LORD looks at the heart."*
>
> 1 SAMUEL 16:7

How's the condition of your heart? Good or not so good? If discipline is what helps someone get to where they want to be and keeps them from ending up someplace they don't, then what disciplines have you incorporated into your life to keep you on track? There's got to be a goal in mind, an objective to reach, an expectation to meet. Perhaps a new year can usher in a new mindset to help you grasp what you've been wanting for a long time.

Your family members don't just need you—they want you involved in their lives. Changing just a few small things in your habits might enable you to alter the destiny of your family, get to where you'd like to be, and keep you from someplace you don't want to end up.

It begins with a fresh start. Perhaps today is that day. Fresh start, new heart! Happy New Year!

"Forget the former things; do not dwell on the past."

ISAIAH 43:18

New beginnings are important for us all: a fresh start, a second chance, a resolution to be different. And it all begins with you. As Paul reminds us, "Forgetting what is behind and straining toward what is ahead, I press on toward the goal to win the prize for which God has called me" (Philippians 3:13–14). Can you do that? Can you give a new chance to anyone in your family who has "blown it"? Even if they blow it again, do what you can to offer them the hand of grace—just as God has done for you. Happy New Year, folks. I pray that this is a wonderful year for you and yours!

*"So do not fear, for I am with you; do not be
dismayed, for I am your God.
I will strengthen you and help you; I will
uphold you with my righteous right hand."*

ISAIAH 41:10

This is the time for a fresh start for you and your teens. It could be a time when you let go of some old rules, begin some new traditions, and set some new expectations. The point is this: you have the opportunity stop some of those old ways that haven't really been that effective. Your teen needs a chance to begin again and will appreciate a fresh start. They long for permission to move to the next level of relationship, which means you have to stop some old habits and begin working on some new opportunities. What is keeping you from turning the page to close the chapter of last year? And what is keeping you from beginning a new chapter of your family? Change happens when there is a deliberate intent to change directions. Take a few moments to ask yourself, "What's going to be different about this new year?"

So we fix our eyes not on what is seen, but on what is unseen, since what is seen is temporary, but what is unseen is eternal.

2 CORINTHIANS 4:18

There's no question that school is valuable. But there are more important things in life than academics: your child's integrity, learning to respect those in authority, respecting the family, understanding the value of a dollar, knowing where they sit with God, and thinking of themselves less often. I guarantee that if you help your teen in these areas, their grades will be fine. And in the process, they might just learn the value of academics.

As you pay attention and put effort into helping your teen "get their life together," you'll find that some of the building blocks will just fall into place. By focusing on the bigger issues—what really matters—the smaller issues will take care of themselves.

> *"My command is this: Love each*
> *other as I have loved you."*
>
> JOHN 15:12

Communication shuts down for a reason. Whether that breakdown has happened over a period of time or because of a particular action, it's important for an attitude of humility and kindness to prevail for there to be any resolution. Resolving conflict is never easy, but it's necessary for relationships to grow deeper.

If everything that comes to you has first passed through the hands of God, then what has come to you now is a small trial that will ultimately make your relationship stronger and healthier.

Here's a first step: admit any wrongdoing. You too, dads. I know it's hard for you to admit you're wrong, but it's essential to look at the log in your own eye before looking at the speck in your teen's eye. Don't let a "log jam" get in the way of a relationship with your teen.

Children's children are a crown to the aged,
and parents are the pride of their children.

PROVERBS 17:6

You have a role in the life of your teenage grandkids. They have a deep need for you. How you engage with them during their teens will determine whether you play an active role in their lives and meet their need to have someone who will give them perspective and listen to their hearts.

You have a choice of whether you will accept the role that God has purposely given you. He is allowing you to live longer so you can influence your grandkids. So go make some incredible memories with them, knowing that your life will have an amazing impact.

Love must be sincere. Hate what
is evil; cling to what is good.

ROMANS 12:9

*P*erfection doesn't exist, and fakeness can be sniffed out from a mile away. Teens want you to be real. Authenticity can be conveyed by being full of grace. It is voiced by speaking truth in love. It is recognized by admitting failures, laughing at yourself, and sharing lessons learned from mistakes. Many times it's speaking your thoughts and struggles when others are hiding theirs. It's doing what is right when it would be easier to do wrong.

Your teens long for a relationship that is real, honest, frank, and sincere. One that is humble and kind. One that considers others to be more important than yourself. They long for relationships that are authentic and genuine.

A gentle answer turns away wrath, but
a harsh word stirs up anger.
PROVERBS 15:1

*I*f you find yourself in occasional battles with your teen, know that many of these clashes have nothing to do with you. Oftentimes the conflict provides an opportunity for your child to release some of their pent-up pressure. Keep that in mind when you want to return fire. Many times a gentle answer turns away an angry teen, and giving no response at all can quiet the battlefront. If the fight is not about you, then don't let a little "steam release" ruin your much-needed relationship with your child.

Now, don't let your teen become disrespectful; that can damage as well. Your approach is key in affirming your commitment to your teen, as many battles can be won before the argument even starts.

*Do nothing out of selfish ambition or vain
conceit. Rather, in humility value others above
yourselves, not looking to your own interests
but each of you to the interests of the others.*

PHILIPPIANS 2:3–4

*D*o I really have to tell you that teens are inherently selfish? Of course they are—we've raised them that way. If we continue doing everything for them, keeping them from assuming personal responsibility, and jumping every time they demand we leap, we are dooming them in their future dating, marriage, and parental relationships.

I'm not saying your child should think less of themselves, but I am encouraging you to help your teen think of themselves less often. It's not always about them. You are key in helping your teen realize the need to put God and others first and break the pattern of selfishness that leads only to greater pain in life.

*A person's wisdom yields patience; it is
to one's glory to overlook an offense.*

PROVERBS 19:11

All of you parents know that you're going to get hurt once in a while during the adolescent years. Most of the time it happens because of a teen's curiosity, ignorance of good advice, or their own quest for independence. These wounds heal a little easier than offenses that are intentional and blatant. Both situations call for being gracious and continuing to offer your love and relationship when hurt feelings would suggest a different approach.

Loving when you've been offended is tough. But that is what grace is all about. It's letting your teen know that there is nothing they can do to make you love them less, and there is nothing they can do to make you love them more—just the way God loves us.

*Be completely humble and gentle; be
patient, bearing with one another in
love. Make every effort to keep the unity of
the Spirit through the bond of peace.*

EPHESIANS 4:2–3

Your teens need to be given the opportunity to flex their decision-making muscles and learn how to make wise choices so they're able to handle the "heavy stuff" later in life. If they aren't allowed to make mistakes during their adolescence, they'll make them later in life when you aren't around to speak truth into their lives and help them learn from those much-needed mistakes and consequences.

Loosen up a little. Give them a little more freedom and let them have a little more responsibility to succeed and to fail, because this is where most of their learning will happen. Remember, you, as the quarterback, are to train up your child, and that means letting them "run with the ball" and take charge of their life.

If any of you lacks wisdom, you should ask
God, who gives generously to all without
finding fault, and it will be given to you.

JAMES 1:5

*L*oss is tough, and the resulting emptiness in our lives impacts all those around us. We all have the tendency to gloss over our losses, but in doing so, we sometimes ignore the mighty work of God Himself to fill those voids created by everyday life. Let me assure you of this: your teen will find their own solutions for filling those empty spots in their life if you don't give them edifying alternatives. Get to the heart of the issue. Don't let your child's behavior determine your actions; instead, be determined to help them see the impact of loss in their own life.

*And let us consider how we may spur one another
on toward love and good deeds, not giving up
meeting together, as some are in the habit of
doing, but encouraging one another—and all
the more as you see the Day approaching.*

HEBREWS 10:24-25

*P*arents often ask me how to counter the negative effects this culture is having on their teens. My answer is that there's never been a greater need for relationship in the lives of your children. What your tween, teen, or young adult really needs is something only you can offer: your time, relationship, wisdom, value, and experience. Parents who spend time building deep and lasting relationships with their children—from their preteen years all the way through young adulthood—can greatly counter the harmful effects of this culture.

They desire a relationship with you more than you'll ever know.

Your word is a lamp for my feet, a light on my path.

PSALM 119:105

I pray that the eyes of your heart may be filled with light—light to see beyond the darkness you feel is engulfing your heart, light to guide you on your current path, light to illuminate the goodness of God's plan in your situation. There's always a bigger picture, always something to learn. Everything that comes to you has first passed through the hands of God. He doesn't waste time, and His purpose is to mold you more and more into His image. Hold on, dear friend. The Lord delights in those who fear Him and put their hope in His unfailing love.

*Start children off on the way they should go, and
even when they are old they will not turn from it.*

PROVERBS 22:6

Your kids are either aware of the challenges they will face in this life, or they're in the middle of one now and don't know how to handle the world that's been given to them. So help them get ready for the inevitable obstacles they'll face. Our job as parents is to protect, provide, and please, but it's also to prepare our children for the next stage of life so that they might be ready to handle what the world will toss at them in their coming days.

If you're hesitant to expose your children to more of life as they get older, remember this: the seeds you have sown into their life will come to fruition, and you can trust that God will continue to watch over their life well beyond your involvement.

JANUARY 16

"A new command I give you: Love one another. As I have loved you, so you must love one another."

JOHN 13:34

Teens are selfish. That's just as true today as when you and I were that age. We just see it more clearly now. Our teens don't care because they don't know what caring looks like; their depth of peer relationships remains rather shallow. It's up to you to teach them about how to care for others. How you care for them will determine how they care for others. The empathy you show to others will also determine their level of empathy. How you relate will determine how they relate. Help them learn that life isn't all about them. It's a lesson that will stay with them for a lifetime.

Create in me a pure heart, O God, and
renew a steadfast spirit within me.

PSALM 51:10

You've had your time for your teen to listen to you; now is the time for you to listen to them. The problem of shallow relationships in your teen's life can be eliminated only by a deeper relationship with you as a parent, not as another friend. Now, if you yourself are caught up in the world of appearance, it's time to start showing your kids that who you are on the inside is much more significant than what's on the outside—that a person's heart is more important than looks, character is more valuable than performance, and who a person is has priority over what a person does.

Go have a conversation with your teen, and instead of just hearing their words, listen to their heart.

The words of the reckless pierce like swords,
but the tongue of the wise brings healing.

PROVERBS 12:18

onflict is going to happen in the course of training your teen. It's inevitable, so get ready! This is your opportunity to share your values and beliefs with your child in a very genuine and real way. When your values clash or inappropriate behaviors present themselves, look at these as chances to convey what you really believe, to transfer the wisdom you have gathered in your heart, and to share the love that's been shared with you. You can never be more Christlike than when you lovingly pursue and listen to the hearts of those who disagree with you. Conflict is a precursor to change, so take advantage of the opportunity.

JANUARY 19

With their mouths the godless
destroy their neighbors, but through
knowledge the righteous escape.

PROVERBS 11:9

We've all been bullied at some time in our life, haven't we? We've all felt disappointment and heartache because of careless words that have been tossed at us or insensitive comments and actions that embarrass or shame us. Well, it's happening with your kids—especially if they're teenagers. Sensitivity to one's appearance in the teen culture is at an all-time high, and painful words flow like a raging tsunami. You hold the key to unlocking the heart of your child and helping them understand this harsh world. Spend some time talking with your teens and creating the openness to discuss the hurts they experience in life. It all begins with you!

God is our refuge and strength, an
ever-present help in trouble.

PSALM 46:1

When a teen is struggling, it's tough—for mom, for dad, and for everyone else in the family. Let me encourage you about your defiant one at home. What you see is not the issue. There may be inappropriate behavior that needs to be corralled, but the real issue is one of the heart. The behavior you see is a symptom of some other problem that goes a lot deeper than defiance. So address both.

Encourage a change in behavior *and* start pursuing the heart of your child. Your loving participation in your teen's life will eventually win out, and this period of defiance will become a thing of the past.

*There is a time for everything, and a season
for every activity under the heavens.*

ECCLESIASTES 3:1

Do you think that asking questions can cause someone to think a little differently?

Do you believe that God has placed you in your child's
life for a purpose? Do you think He's placed your child
in your life for a reason? Do you think God really knows
when a sparrow falls to the earth? Do you think He's ever
not listened to you? Has He ever not heard your cries? Has
your child ever felt the same way toward you? If that's true,
let me ask you a question: What can you do to change the
way you engage with your teen? When do you think that
needs to start?

Wouldn't today be a good day to start asking questions?

I pray that the eyes of your heart may be
enlightened in order that you may know
the hope to which he has called you.

EPHESIANS 1:18

There's nothing easy about suicide—for anyone. It's a punch in the stomach and is every parent's and grandparent's worst nightmare. It's always a surprise that catches parents off guard. I've never heard people say, "I knew this was going to happen." My prayer is that God would help us all as parents to pick up on the messages our kids want us to hear and that we would not ignore their silent screams for understanding and calls for help in a hopeless world. Let us pray that God would help us see with the eyes of our heart and know, and help others to know, the hope He has called us to.

Teach us to number our days, that we
may gain a heart of wisdom.

PSALM 90:12

During this time of dark, cold winter, most of us eagerly await the warm weather that summer brings. But the summer months can be either the best of times or the worst of times. A little bit of planning will ensure that you'll end the summer longing for more time with your teens. Make sure that all in your family know the expectations, have shared experiences, and are looking for more opportunities to engage. Instead of sending your kid off to do something with others, look for ways to do some things together. The memories of a lifetime are often created in the all-but-forgotten years of adolescence, so take advantage of the time you have with your teen and make this summer one that is magnificent, meaningful, and memorable.

The king said to Daniel,
"Surely your God is the God of gods and the
Lord of kings and a revealer of mysteries, for
you were able to reveal this mystery."

DANIEL 2:47

If your child is always angry and seems to never show respect, chances are something is going on in the life of your teen. I'm sure that your parents don't know everything that happened in your life when you were in high school, so I doubt that you know everything that's happened in the life of your child. Something might be eating at your teen; perhaps something you are doing might be provoking the behavior you see. If it is, acknowledge and pledge to rectify the situation if you are at fault. And if your child is just becoming one of those "mean kids," then appropriate consequences need to be established and enforced. Learning to show respect and developing ways to control anger are paramount to your child's future success—and your sanity.

*Therefore encourage one another and build
each other up, just as in fact you are doing.*

1 THESSALONIANS 5:11

There's nothing quite like a struggling teen to create distance between a husband and wife: emotions are raw and relationships become strained. That's why it's important not to let the struggle of one ruin a marriage of two.

If you can identify the problem, then commit to not letting it take you down. Make a promise to each other to stay focused and get help from two places: first, from someone a little older who understands and, second, from a peer group of couples who can support you during this time.

Don't let a short-term struggle ruin your long-term relationship.

For all have sinned and fall
short of the glory of God.
ROMANS 3:23

Nobody is perfect, so stop trying to come off as someone who is. Your teen already knows that you aren't. The desire for and appearance of perfection when your child was younger worked in your "teaching model." But it doesn't in your teen's "training model." Now is the time to make a shift if your parenting style is sending the contradictory messages of "I'll accept you when you appear perfect" and "I'll love you equally when you show me your imperfection." Tonight, share one thing about yourself that lets your teen know that it's okay to struggle, to make mistakes, and not have it all together.

You might just be surprised how your teen will appreciate hearing that you're normal—just like them.

Do not be deceived: God cannot be mocked.
A man reaps what he sows.

GALATIANS 6:7

*D*on't underestimate the ability of the seeds you've sown into the life of your teen to come to life at a time when it is needed most. When a teen struggles with their faith, it becomes an issue of God's work and timing, not yours.

Let me encourage you to trust God's timing. Trust the seeds you have sown in your teen. And trust that the faith-filled life they've seen in you will continue to be a reflection of not only your witness but also your "withness" as you move toward them at a time when they are moving away from what they have been taught.

*Be kind and compassionate to one
another, forgiving each other,
just as in Christ God forgave you.*

EPHESIANS 4:32

Scripture tells us, "A brother wronged is more unyielding than a fortified city" (Proverbs 18:19). When we are hurt, it's hard to move toward the offender. Whether we hurt others or are hurt in our relationships, we must show that the love we have been given can overcome the awkwardness and uneasiness we feel in approaching those whom God has placed in our lives.

Perhaps there's a person for you to call this afternoon—someone who has hurt you or someone you have hurt. Forgiveness is giving up hope that you'll ever have a better past. Grace is moving toward a person when you have every right to walk away. It's treating them just as God has treated you.

*So in everything, do to others what
you would have them do to you.*

MATTHEW 7:12

The way someone approaches you makes all the difference, doesn't it? I guarantee that if you approach your teen in the same way you approached them during their elementary school years, there will be a breakdown of relationship. Instead of lecture, approach with discussion. Instead of giving answers, ask questions. Instead of giving more information, approach with wisdom. Instead of teaching, shift your parenting style toward training.

Your teen wants connection with you and longs to grow a relationship that will mature and adjust along with the ever-changing demands of the culture in which they live. And they need your help. Make the commitment to parenting your teen the way that God parents you: full of grace and full of truth.

*But the wisdom that comes from heaven is first of
all pure; then peace-loving, considerate, submissive,
full of mercy and good fruit, impartial and sincere.*

JAMES 3:17

Were there things during your teen years that you later found weren't really important at all? Do you think there might be things today that won't really matter in the days ahead? Sure there are. The hard part is determining what is important now and what is not so that the minor issues don't confuse the major issues.

Pick your battles wisely. It's okay to lose a few battles if you know you're going to win the war. If giving up a little is going to get you a lot, then make a sacrifice for the greater good. It may be a good battle to let go of. Love well, listen much, and approach your child with humility and kindness.

May these words of my mouth and this meditation
of my heart be pleasing in your sight, LORD.

PSALM 19:14

*I*f there are issues within your family, it's important to deal with those things now instead of just "waiting it out" and allowing situations to correct themselves. Your desire to resolve conflict lets your teen know they are valued and that you are not afraid to deal with difficult situations.

The message that your teen will hear is "You are worth fighting for." To ignore the need to resolve conflict sends the opposite message to your child. Unresolved conflict only returns later in life when consequences are greater and more relationships are affected, so commit to resolving anything that is getting in the way of your relationship with your teen.

Do not exasperate your children; instead, bring
them up in the training and instruction of the Lord.
EPHESIANS 6:4

What was effective in the way you were parented isn't necessarily the way to parent your kids. As a matter of fact, if you try to parent the same way you were raised, it might just be provoking your child to wrath and creating more problems. If you have a discipline problem, you have a relationship problem. The way you're trying to relate with your teen might just be antiquated and may fail to work in today's adolescent culture.

Look and see if your style is working. Ask your kids. If it isn't, commit to adding some new tools to your parenting toolbox. Your teens long to connect with you, and if a change in your parenting style can bring that about, make it your priority.

Above all, love each other deeply, because
love covers over a multitude of sins.

1 PETER 4:8

*D*o you get frustrated when you don't see change happening within your family? Are you waiting for your teen to "make her move," or are you trying to figure out what you might need to accomplish so that the atmosphere of your home will allow that change to happen?

Teens want change—constantly. Very few are comfortable to keep doing the same thing over and over like the movie *Groundhog Day*. They want to see change; they just don't know how to get there. It's your role as a parent to develop an environment that welcomes change and adapts along with your teen to meet their new needs. Consider how hard it is to change yourself, and you'll understand what little chance you have in trying to change others. Change begins in an atmosphere that welcomes transformation.

*The LORD is close to the brokenhearted and
saves those who are crushed in spirit.*

PSALM 34:18

*P*ain is never easy. The feeling of not having it all together is particularly difficult, especially for moms who have done everything they know how to do and for dads who have always been able to "fix" their family.

Somewhere in our brokenness, God creates a longing for something different, something that might change the direction of your family. C. S. Lewis said that "pain is God's megaphone to a deaf world." Well, does He have your attention? If so, take advantage of this time to figure out your role in the struggle within your family and set your goal on resolving those issues that have burdened you for years. Now is the time!

"Whoever has ears, let them hear."

MATTHEW 11:15

Your teens are longing for you to listen and understand. And if you won't listen, they'll find someone else who will. May I encourage you to step up in your communication? Listen to understand, not to respond. What you'll find is that as your teen is heard, they'll begin to listen to you as well, and you'll begin to have an exchange of ideas and thoughts. So put down the phone and pick up the conversation that your teen so desperately needs and longs to have with you. Conversation does not begin by opening your mouth—it begins with ears eager to listen.

*The LORD is a refuge for the oppressed, a
stronghold in times of trouble.*

PSALM 9:9

*D*epression is a silent destroyer of hopes and dreams, and it has the potential to change the very character of your child and how they engage with peers and with you. Don't shame them for not being able to "handle it." That will only push them deeper into depression. Make your home a place of hope, a place where your child finds encouragement and affirmation, a place that allows rest from the culture that seems to be taking a toll on them. And by all means, find some help outside the home if necessary.

Take depression seriously and act quickly if you see signs of it in your teen.

"In the same way, let your light shine before others, that they may see your good deeds and glorify your Father in heaven."

MATTHEW 5:16

You know that actions speak louder than words. It's not what you say but what you do that really counts. Words express who you want to be; actions speak of who you are. The adolescent years are a time when teens are searching for wisdom, hoping to take what they know to be true and live it out in their life. That's where they need you. They gather wisdom through observation, reflection, and experience. If the Christian life is more caught than taught, let them observe wisdom through your lifestyle and the way you pour your life into them, not only by your witness but by your "withness"!

Give careful thought to the paths for your
feet and be steadfast in all your ways.

PROVERBS 4:26

Can I say this? Quit giving your kids everything. You're keeping them from coming to their senses. Your teen is capable of handling a lot more than you think, so give them a chance. Remember, you are to train them up and prepare them to function positively in their next stage of life. It feels good to give gifts, but if it's not beneficial to the one who receives that gift, you're participating in something that will eventually bring harm to their future relationships. Provision can quickly turn into enabling, and that enabling only postpones maturity and the development of responsibility. Begin your change today, letting your teens know you owe them nothing but want to give them everything that's best for them.

All Scripture is God-breathed and is useful for
teaching, rebuking, correcting and training in
righteousness, so that the servant of God may
be thoroughly equipped for every good work.

2 TIMOTHY 3:16–17

Kids who struggle are deceitful and will probably lie to you in the process of figuring out what is going on in their life. But they do it for a reason. It's usually because they don't trust you, are fearful of consequences, or are trying to project an image that you will accept. If so, it's your job to create an atmosphere of honesty where open communication is safe and welcome. Begin by asking yourself some questions: Why does my teen lie to me? Do I need to change my approach? Is there something I'm doing wrong? Don't let your child's lying keep them from the relationship they need the most to work through this bad habit—their relationship with you!

*Commit to the LORD whatever you
do, and he will establish your plans.*

PROVERBS 16:3

There's no question that our teens live in a broken world. And that brokenness sometimes spills over into their lives. Whether curiosity gets the best of them or they choose to partake for other reasons, it's important for you to realize that an opportunity to consume alcohol will present itself prior to their graduation from high school. So be prepared.

Have conversations that invite dialogue about alcohol. Let your teen know what you believe about underage drinking. Set the consequences for inappropriate behavior. Above everything else, make sure your teen knows that's there's nothing he or she can do that will make you love them more or less.

Demonstrate a love that supersedes alcohol use or any other bad choice they'll ever make.

*In everything set them an example
by doing what is good.*

TITUS 2:7

Respect is something we all want. And our teens want it just as much as we do. This presents a challenge for most of us: we have to give it before we get it. I know, I know, it's a shift in the way we look at the roles we play as parents, but it's key that we understand the need to shift our expectations in light of today's adolescent culture.

So keep offering respect and move toward your teen when you feel disrespected. Get to the core issue of that disrespect. The example you set by giving respect when it's not reciprocated is a golden nugget of truth that will never be forgotten, and it will eventually show your child the value of respect within your family.

Let your eyes look straight ahead;
fix your gaze directly before you.
PROVERBS 4:25

*I*f you do everything for your teen, they won't learn how to handle the things they need to do when they're out on their own. I know you want to have a deeper relationship with your kids, but you'll never get there by doing everything for them, making excuses for inexcusable behavior, and rescuing them from their mistakes and poor choices.

They can make it, just as you did. In the long run, they'll love you for not swooping in to save them. They may hate you in the moment, but encouraging them to see the bigger picture will help your teen become responsible, gain wisdom, and develop the ability to make good choices and better decisions.

Be devoted to one another in love.

ROMANS 12:10

A change of season is an opportunity to usher in a change of heart. Perhaps this summer is one that can be memorable in the life of your teen and your family. You only have a few of them before things start getting really busy and your teen moves to the next stage of life.

Don't live a life of regrets. When you get to your child's wedding, my hope is that you'll have a bucketload of memories to talk about at the rehearsal dinner. Today is the day to start making those memories. Take a chance, take a risk, do something new that you've never done before. And do it with your teens. It may just be an experience that will change their life—and yours!

And the God of all grace, who called you to
his eternal glory in Christ, after you have
suffered a little while, will himself restore you
and make you strong, firm and steadfast.

1 PETER 5:10

We've all been lost, haven't we? And I bet that when you were lost, you didn't really need someone nagging you about how you got lost, lecturing you about what you should have done, or reminding you that you're off the path.

Chances are you needed someone to encourage you without using the word encouragement. And chances are that you wanted someone to come alongside you to walk with you and together find your way back to where you knew you needed to be.

Your teen is no different. They're not being rebellious—they're just lost. And just like you, they want to be found. So show some grace and be a beacon of direction instead of a wall of correction.

*Love is patient, love is kind. It does not envy,
it does not boast, it is not proud. It does not dishonor
others, it is not self-seeking, it is not easily angered, it
keeps no record of wrongs. Love does not delight in
evil but rejoices with the truth. It always protects,
always trusts, always hopes, always perseveres. Love
never fails. . . . And now these three remain: faith,
hope and love. But the greatest of these is love.*

1 CORINTHIANS 13:4–8, 13

Your relationship with your spouse will define what love is in the hearts of your children. If moms instill a sense of value into the life of children and dads validate that worth, that is the example your teen will follow.

So, how is your love life? What do your teens see in the way you treat your neighbors, your coworkers, your family, or other people in your church? More importantly, what do they see when they observe their mom and dad's relationship? Or Grandma and Grandpa's?

You're being watched. You're setting the standard. You're giving your children a taste of how God loves them. You can have a lot of faith and you can embrace hope, but I would encourage you to always ask those around you how you can love better.

He heals the brokenhearted and
binds up their wounds.

PSALM 147:3

Nothing leaves a parent feeling more alone than when their teen moves in a direction contrary to what a mom or dad desires. In the midst of this feeling, remember the Scripture: "Never will I leave you; never will I forsake you" (Hebrews 13:5).

God won't abandon you, even when you feel that your teen has.

Loneliness is a tough place to be, and conflict is a precursor to change. Both statements are true, and both are hard. But it's in these tough times that God promises to give wisdom to those who ask. He promises to never forget the needy and assures us that the hope of the afflicted will never perish. We can be confident that He will turn our mourning into dancing, our sadness into joy, and our ashes into beauty.

You are not alone.

"Do to others as you would have them do to you."

LUKE 6:31

The connection you make with your teen is the most important relationship they will ever have. They not only need you; they desperately want you. Do what you have to do to make sure that the relationship with your teen is your priority, and they'll make sure you are theirs.

You've spent years sowing seeds of truth into the life of your children; now cultivate the soil of their life with your relationship, and do so in a way that gives them a taste of the character of God. This means you parent them the way that God parents you!

So be intentional in your efforts to build a relationship, just as God does with you.

*Do your best to present yourself to
God as one approved, a worker who
does not need to be ashamed.*

2 TIMOTHY 2:15

Your teens really do want to have conversations with you. But if productive discussions aren't happening, the ball is in your court to change your approach and find new ways to engage with your teen.

Your greatest tool of communication is the example you set for your teens. Remember, the Christian life is caught more than taught, so make sure your life is a precursor to the words that will come out of your mouth. As Proverbs states, even a fool appears wise when he keeps his mouth shut. Are you hearing me? It's hard to listen when words are coming out of your mouth.

When you learn to listen with the sole intent of hearing your son or daughter's heart, they'll eventually let you into theirs.

*Let us not become weary in doing
good, for at the proper time we will
reap a harvest if we do not give up.*

GALATIANS 6:9

Have you gotten used to the fact that life hasn't been turning out the way you thought it would? For most parents, it doesn't. That doesn't mean that all is lost; it just means that things are going to look a little different than you anticipated.

While it can be difficult, it's important to maintain a relationship with your teen who may be conveying a message that's hard to hear. Don't let your son or daughter's viewpoints or actions determine your desire to move toward them. Don't grow weary in doing good, for in due time you will reap an abundant harvest if you continue to faithfully sow.

*Those whom I love I rebuke and
discipline. So be earnest and repent.*

REVELATION 3:19

Respect is one of the most important character traits to build into the life of your child. In their earlier years, you developed this attribute; now you have to coach it. First look to see if you're provoking their disrespect in any way. This is where you look at the log rather than stare at the speck.

Then be respectful in your approach. I've always found that the best way to address disrespect is to approach with respect.

Your continually and deliberately addressing their lack of respect will soon melt the heart of your teen and move them back into the loving relationship you both long for.

*Do not turn to the right or the
left; keep your foot from evil.*
PROVERBS 4:27

*T*eens learn best by making mistakes and suffering a
bit from the consequences. They remember lessons
when there are consequences because they are then able to
figure out for themselves if the punishment was worth the
pain. Set up your rules and consequences in your home so
that your teen understands the results of their poor choices.

Disciplining your child means keeping them on a
path that is righteous and healthy and keeping them from
straying onto a path that leads to destruction. Reward good
choices and have attention-getting consequences for the
bad ones. Over time, your child will learn by their own
choices, and you'll be freed up to develop a deeper and
stronger relationship.

No discipline seems pleasant at the time, but
painful. Later on, however, it produces
a harvest of righteousness and peace for
those who have been trained by it.

HEBREWS 12:11

Discipline has never really been any fun, except for maybe a drill sergeant. But it never will be pleasant for you. Yet it is necessary. Think of it like this: I hate stop signs and stoplights, but I wouldn't want to live without them.

And so it is with discipline. You might hate it, but it's needed. So be sure to make the discipline about your child's needs and not about your own frustration and anger. And start early; as Scripture says, "Discipline your children, for in that there is hope" (Proverbs 19:18).

Your child may never thank you for disciplining them, but he or she will thank you for your willingness to participate in their training and help make them into the person God has designed them to be.

Teach me knowledge and good judgment,
for I trust your commands.

PSALM 119:66

*I*n his book *Wild at Heart*, John Eldredge wrote, "Deep in his heart, every man longs for a battle to fight, an adventure to live, and a beauty to rescue." I think Mr. Eldredge would agree that video games offer this opportunity for young men and are a way to pass time for our young ladies.

The problem with video games is not the game itself but rather the opportunity cost associated with it. When teens are absorbed in a video game they are forgoing the pursuit of normal relational longings that are achieved through genuine personal interaction and real social settings.

As a parent, you can initiate a change by limiting the game time to a reasonable amount and encouraging and providing other ways of social interaction. Your teen was created to be in relationship with others and may need some help learning to engage appropriately.

The tongue has the power of life and death,
and those who love it will eat its fruit.

PROVERBS 18:21

Your teen is searching for a safe place to share their heart, and you can add immense value to their lives when you spend quality time listening to their ideas, thoughts, hurts, and complaints. You must be the one to create the welcoming atmosphere by offering wisdom for their life, something they can embrace and value. Hear this: they want to be able to communicate with you. So ask questions that encourage them to share their emotions and deeply held thoughts. Emotions open the door to your teen's heart, so take advantage of the invitation as you walk into a new relationship of conversation that will last a lifetime.

Finally, brothers and sisters, rejoice!
Strive for full restoration, encourage one another,
be of one mind, live in peace.
And the God of love and peace will be with you.

2 CORINTHIANS 13:11

Home is where the heart is, right? My prayer for you is that you would work hard to create an atmosphere where your teen can know that home is the one place of refuge and retreat where he or she can be refreshed. Teens live in a tough culture and are constantly searching for a place of rest where relationship is more important than rules and where connection rates above correction. Maybe it's time to do a little home remodeling, to update some old ways of operating so your weary ones feel welcomed at home and learn from the gentle and humble relationship they find in you.

The soothing tongue is a tree of life,
but a perverse tongue crushes the spirit.

PROVERBS 15:4

Believe it or not, how your daughter feels about herself as she transitions into adolescence comes directly from you and how you've handled situations in her earlier years. Your affirmation of who she is and the value you instill make a huge difference as your daughter enters her teen years. In light of that, be careful, for she's hanging onto every word and watching every action that affects her belief about herself. Limit your criticism, increase your praise, "have her back" when needed, and encourage her even when she makes mistakes. Value her by listening and being involved in her life. And when she messes up, make sure she knows that there is nothing that can detract from the love you have for her.

Stop listening to instruction, my son, and you
will stray from the words of knowledge.

PROVERBS 19:27

You've got a choice to make. You've got to determine where you land on allowing your teenage son or daughter to date in this sexually charged culture. Perhaps you don't need to focus as much on controlling the "ifs" and "whens" of dating for your teen; maybe your priority needs to be training them to engage with the opposite sex in a way that is appropriate and in line with the principles and values you've taught them.

Dating isn't what it used to be. And the culture isn't the same as when we were growing up. So the standards that you've been holding onto for years may need to be reviewed to ensure they're practical, protective, and allowing your teen to pursue knowing more and more about relationships with the opposite sex. Your guidelines in this area will one day determine who your future son- or daughter-in-law will be, so be wise!

Discipline your children,
and they will give you peace;
they will bring you the delights you desire.

PROVERBS 29:17

Sometimes it's hard to believe that teens want structure. But they really do! Especially when it outlines
the future freedoms they'll have and the privileges they'll
receive by following a process that you can use to develop
their responsibility and maturity. It takes a little work, but
in the long run it provides an atmosphere where your relationship can flourish because you're all working together
for the same goals: independence, freedom, letting them
make decisions, and helping them to embrace the values
and principles that you've taught all their life. It's called
parenting—parenting your kids just as your heavenly
Father parents you.

Rejoice in the Lord always.
I will say it again: Rejoice!

PHILIPPIANS 4:4

It's always hard to let go of something you have invested so much of your time in. Our kids are no exception. Yet it's essential we keep in mind that, in one sense, our teens aren't ours. In reality, our role is not only to love them but to prepare them for their next stage of life. One metric of your effectiveness as a parent can be the simple observation of how they function once they leave your home. See the importance of training? If you get this right about loosening the reins, you will enjoy the days to come far more than those that have passed.

Set your minds on things above,
not on earthly things.

COLOSSIANS 3:2

When a teen starts to spin out of control, a parent's first response is to fight back, forgetting that the bad behavior is really just a symptom of something else going on in the child's life. It's hard to see, and that's why Scripture encourages us to look with the "eyes of our heart." Don't spend too much time looking at the obvious; focus instead on the motivation of the behavior you see. Now is the time to deal with the issues driving your child's inappropriate actions. All behavior is goal oriented. What is your teen trying to tell you through his or her behavior?

MARCH 1

*"If anyone causes one of these little ones—those
who believe in me—to stumble, it would be better
for them if a large millstone were hung around
their neck and they were thrown into the sea."*

MARK 9:42

I'd never wish a divorce on my worst enemy. It's a tough
position for the husband and wife, but I think it's an even
tougher spot for a child, who really longs to have a family
with a mom and a dad. If your home has gone through the
devastation of a divorce and you find yourself "splitting"
the parenting role, I would encourage you to hold to what
you know to be true and define new rules and boundaries
that will allow your relationship with your child to flourish.

This Scripture would remind everyone, married,
divorced, or going through a divorce of the responsibility
we have to consider the impact of any of our decisions so
we don't cause more problems for our children as we work
through ours.

It's a tough spot, so hold on to your faith, your relationship with your teen, and your mission to be to your child
who God has been to you.

*Love must be sincere. Hate what
is evil; cling to what is good.*

ROMANS 12:9

Chances are your son has already seen porn on the
Internet. Dads, you have a critical role in training your
son how to handle something that is so powerful, attractive,
and readily available. My encouragement would be not to
shame your son for something that has become somewhat
"normal" to this age group. Shame only pushes someone
further into sin. Instead, outline a path for your son, hold
him accountable, and let him hold you accountable as well.

Commit to tackling together the problem that is before
you. Dads, your frank and honest discussions, coupled with
your intent to "do battle together," will draw your relationship with your son even closer than it is today.

That elephant will only go away with honest and frank
discussions, all shared in love and humility, as you talk
about the harder subjects facing teens today.

*I will instruct you and teach you in
the way you should go; I will counsel
you with my loving eye on you.*

PSALM 32:8

*E*very one of us wants to protect our kids from a world of negative influence, and we all want to train up a child in the way he should go. You can choose to either raise your kids in a zoo or prepare them to survive in the jungle. I would suggest the latter. Your involvement with your kids is wonderful. Your commitment of time and effort is honorable. And your sacrifice to make sure your kids are not negatively influenced is to be praised. But make sure you're preparing them for the world they will live in, not the one you want them to live in.

*Like apples of gold in settings of
silver is a ruling rightly given.*

PROVERBS 25:11

I wonder if your teen is hearing what you intend to say or if they don't have a clue about the love language you are speaking. Truth be told, there are many different ways that a child feels love. Your goal as a parent is to make sure you're "speaking their language" so you can accurately convey what you precisely feel. What is your teen's love language? Are you limiting it to the five languages that you know? Or are you willing to expand your vocabulary and broaden your language skills? Or maybe learn some new ways to love your child the way they'd love to be loved.

Learn their language, speak it often, convey your love through actions, and don't hesitate to let them know how much you love them.

*"Why do you look at the speck of sawdust
in your brother's eye and pay no attention
to the plank in your own eye?"*

MATTHEW 7:3

We've all blown it at one time or another, haven't we? And there have been times that we haven't quite handled a situation in the best of ways. We've all been there as parents. Well, this is where Scripture reminds us to look at the log in our own eye before looking at the speck in another's. Remember the prayer that says, "Search me, God.... See if there is any offensive way in me" (Psalm 139:23–24)? It's important to constantly examine our own heart and actions so we don't become the cause of our teen's rebellion. You may just be amazed to find that an admission of your own shortcomings will have a way of drawing your teen closer to you.

*For we are God's handiwork, created in
Christ Jesus to do good works, which God
prepared in advance for us to do.*
EPHESIANS 2:10

Adoption is a great thing—until everything takes an
unexpected turn and you begin to question whether
you've done the right thing. Well, let me assure you that
you have. God has placed this child into your family and
grafted him or her into your life for a purpose. Our sovereign
God knew the struggles your child would go through
and knows that you are capable of helping them through
this difficult time.

Hang in there and embrace the opportunity you have
to change the destiny of this child's life. God's plan for your
family is still in place. One day soon you'll see the plan He
put in your heart years ago come to fruition.

But test them all; hold on to what is good.

1 THESSALONIANS 5:21

*L*et me ask you a question: What do you do that bugs your teen to death? Do you know the answer? If not, then today might be the time to sit down and ask that question. And don't take "I don't know" for an answer. We all do things that push our kids away. If you're going to create an atmosphere of relationship that draws your kids closer to you as they get older, then you must find out what you do that's keeping that from happening. Ouch! It might hurt to hear, but the fact that you listen to your child, and act on their observations, might just provide an atmosphere of change that they need in their life as well.

*Keep your tongue from evil and
your lips from telling lies.*

PSALM 34:13

Communication has changed a little bit since we were teens, hasn't it? Of course it has, so we must keep that in mind when we oversee how our children connect with their friends. Yes, we want to protect them from negative influences. But we must also provide ways for our kids to engage and communicate with peers. Learn how your teen's culture makes connections, then determine how to limit and restrict at the right times so you can encourage growth and not defer the development of maturity and responsibility.

Communication has changed, and so the rules you set for cell phones, apps, and Internet access must as well. Encourage connection, but discourage inappropriateness. Spend time having verbal discussions with your teen and teach them to communicate heart to heart.

*Through Jesus, therefore, let us continually
offer to God a sacrifice of praise—the fruit
of lips that openly profess his name.*

HEBREWS 13:15

Sometimes kids and grandkids have a tough time being thankful when they feel so entitled. If this sentiment resonates with you, then know this: you're normal. We all live in an age where kids feel entitled. It's our job to help them break this mentality and develop a sense of self-provision and responsibility. Entitlement has an amazing way of destroying relationships, ruining marriages, and terminating jobs early. Adolescence is a crucial time for changing these thinking patterns, and it's your responsibility to initiate the change you'd like to see in your teen. Kids have always felt entitled, but you can make some changes and help them learn the spirit of thankfulness.

Gracious words are a honeycomb, sweet
to the soul and healing to the bones.
PROVERBS 16:24

*I*s it any surprise that your child lives in a world that prioritizes appearance and performance? In light of that, it's our job to communicate that we value them based on who they are, not what they do. It's letting them know that even on their worst day, your family is better because they're a part of it. It's communicating, in both actions and words, that nothing will ever change your love for them. Show your child the same kind of unconditional love that God shows toward you.

Nevertheless, when we are judged in this way
by the Lord, we are being disciplined so that we
will not be finally condemned with the world.

1 CORINTHIANS 11:32

Scripture tells us that a father disciplines those he loves; reinforcing that discipline is a part of parenting and a way to show love to our children. Discipline is all about showing them the right way to live and helping them understand why it's so important. Discipline is all about them, not us. How do you know that difference? When we make discipline about us, it provokes our kids to wrath. Let me encourage you to sit down with your teen and have a discussion about discipline, letting them know that your intent is to help them walk the path that will lead them to success. Don't wait until everything is falling apart. Have that discussion now.

How much better to get wisdom than
gold, to get insight rather than silver!

PROVERBS 16:16

You may not be as smart as your child, but I can guarantee that you are wiser. And wisdom is what they long for. When conversing with your teen, don't let it turn into a competition based on a constant and nagging transfer of information; instead, engage patiently and calmly by imparting wisdom, something your child lacks. Help them learn that the pursuit of wisdom leads to pleasure, and foolishness leads to pain. You are able to offer the valuable lessons life has taught you, and they will become more and more valuable in the days ahead as your teen realizes being smarter isn't always wiser.

*"But seek first his kingdom and his righteousness,
and all these things will be given to you as well."*

MATTHEW 6:33

*I*f you asked your teen to describe what your goals in
life are, what would they say? Would they know what
you desire out of life, or would they only comment on
what they see? Many times, the image we want to portray
doesn't match up with the actions they see from us. It's not
that what they see is necessarily wrong; you've just got to
remind them of the bigger picture of your life.

Take the time to share with your child the bigger
picture. Let them in on your plan for fulfilling God's calling
on your life, and ask them to be a part of it. You might just
be surprised how they would like to understand the "goal
of the book" rather than just reading "chapter titles." Your
sharing might just trigger a desire for something bigger
in their life and provide that special opportunity to walk
alongside them in a new way.

*Therefore, as we have opportunity, let us
do good to all people, especially to those
who belong to the family of believers.*

GALATIANS 6:10

If you're struggling with your teen, hang in there. All is not lost even though you feel like your teen might be. More than anything else, your teen needs to know that you love them regardless of their behavior or what the situation may look like. The atmosphere you create will be an invitation for your child to return to what he or she knows is right and will begin to form a space where you can share your desires to help them get to a good place. And if your child rejects what you offer, don't grow weary in doing good. In due time, you'll reap if you consistently sow good seeds. Change what you can and offer a new chance. Hope is around the corner.

*A father to the fatherless, a defender
of widows, is God in his holy dwelling.
God sets the lonely in families.*

PSALM 68:5–6

*I*f you have adopted your child, then you know that some of their patterns of thinking and behavior have nothing to do with you. Many times, no matter how much you nurture, it's difficult to change someone's nature. All your efforts have not been in vain. You've sown seeds into the life of your child that will one day bear fruit. When you face the challenges of adoption with your child and help them see how they belong in your family, they will come to understand their past circumstances and embrace the love that you have and offer to them. Adoption is an admirable process, and your efforts do not go unnoticed.

*"Is not wisdom found among the aged?
Does not long life bring understanding?"*

JOB 12:12

Your teen's world is a mess. Chances are good that there are many things you don't understand about their culture—and neither do they. Your commitment to have long discussions, hang out and spend time with them, and offer the wisdom that you have to give will eventually help them navigate through this crazy adolescent culture. While it might be contrary to what you expect, this atmosphere provides the perfect opportunity for you to engage with your teen in ways that others pray for. You are in your teen's life for a reason: to offer them help and hope at a time that they need it most. So buckle down, gain an understanding, and help your teen process and understand their role in this contrary culture.

*For the LORD gives wisdom; from his mouth
come knowledge and understanding.*

PROVERBS 2:6

*I*f you're like me, your first stab at parenting teens probably didn't work too well. Perhaps you've believed that
the style you learned by observation would work on your
teens as it did on you. That's wrong. The adolescent culture
has changed, so you must gain a new understanding of that
world. Mom and Dad, you have to shift from just pleasing,
protecting, and providing for your teen to begin preparing
them for the world they will live in.

You're not wrong in what you're doing; you may just
need to do some things differently so you can accomplish
what you desire and be the mom and dad that your son or
daughter hopes you will become.

The beginning of wisdom is this: Get wisdom.
Though it cost all you have, get understanding.

PROVERBS 4:7

If you have a teen who is struggling, chances are you're carrying around a pretty heavy heart as well. Commit to your spouse that you won't let a child's struggles affect your marriage. And if you're a single parent, don't let your teen drive you crazy. Whatever your situation, I encourage you to get involved with others who are going through something similar so you can be supported by people who have "been there and done that." Get counsel, and don't lean on your own understanding. Ask of God and of other people you know who have gained a wealth of wisdom.

But in fact God has placed the parts in the body,
every one of them, just as he wanted them to be.

1 CORINTHIANS 12:18

*I*f you want your teen to be a leader, you must help make that happen. But before you push them into a role they might not want to be in, ask what they want. Not every position of leadership is the best for every teen.

And remember this: when you're called to be a servant, don't stoop to be a king. Your teen may be one that is content to serve others. They may not want to lead but instead feel comfortable in following. That's not a bad thing when they are following the example of the One who gave His life for all. Provide the opportunity to develop leadership skills, but leave it up to God to determine the place where they fit best. He does a good job at placing people in just the right places.

*Search me, God, and know my heart; test
me and know my anxious thoughts. See
if there is any offensive way in me, and
lead me in the way everlasting.*

PSALM 139:23–24

*I*f you're like me, chances are you do some things that bug your child and may even offend them. It's because you're not perfect. Identifying and admitting those areas of agitation are the first moves to developing a better relationship with your teen.

Don't know what those things are? Ask your teen. Given the right question at the right time, you'll get an answer that can make you a better parent. Pray, *Lord, search me, know my heart, and see if there is any hurtful way in me.* Sometimes, just acknowledging that you're not perfect creates an atmosphere where that imperfect teen of yours feels more comfortable, giving an opportunity for a deeper relationship to form. That's what you want, and it's what your teen needs more than anything.

Give, and it will be given to you. A good measure,
pressed down, shaken together and running
over, will be poured into your lap. For with the
measure you use, it will be measured to you.

LUKE 6:38

Alcohol has been around for a long time, and teens have been taking advantage of it for just as long. But today it has become so available and so permissible. Underage drinking and alcohol abuse are not just happening "over there"; they're happening in your community and in your neighborhood—and maybe even in your own home.

If it is, then you have the opportunity to share your experiences, your wisdom, and your observations with your teen and let them know why you think it's not best that they partake while they live in your home. The stance you take on drinking is important, and your commitment to loving them through their time of curiosity and experimentation is equally as important.

*Every good and perfect gift is from above, coming
down from the Father of the heavenly lights,
who does not change like shifting shadows.*

JAMES 1:17

Your teen is living one life online and another in your home. They can be one person to you and someone completely different when they're online. The Internet fosters anonymity, curiosity, and the opportunity to be who they wish they could be. Make sure you know of their other life.

But here's what I've also found: teens search for those things that they're not receiving at home, things such as value, attention, admiration, respect, and connection. How are you doing in those areas of your relationship with your child? If they don't get it from you, I guarantee they'll get it somewhere else. You are the greatest relationship that your teen will ever have.

Children do not go searching online for needs met at home.

The one who gets wisdom loves life; the one who cherishes understanding will soon prosper.

PROVERBS 19:8

Did you ever think that the issues and situations facing your teen would be as potentially damaging as they are? I'm sure every generation has its challenges, but this generation is experiencing a shift in the way people relate and seek help from one another.

That's where you come in. Your teens need you—your wisdom, your counsel, your time, and your influence. They need these things now more than ever. Even when you think they don't, they do. And I assure you that even though they don't appear to be listening, they are. With that in mind, do whatever it takes to improve your relationship so that you can be that light in their darkness, a ray of hope in their confusion, and a place where they are loved like no other.

*"Whoever can be trusted with very little can also
be trusted with much, and whoever is dishonest
with very little will also be dishonest with much."*

LUKE 16:10

Your teens need your financial help. No, I'm not talking about giving them money; I'm talking about helping them understand the world of finance and how money and credit works. They need to be taught about investments, about how not to spend more than they earn, and about how to make all they can, save all they can, and give all they can.

It's called financial training. And your investment in this area of their life will one day make for a happier marriage and family life as they begin to work and live in a world that demands financial responsibility. Create opportunities for learning and give occasion for your teens to make some financial decisions. It's how they will learn and will see the importance of your counsel.

*"In your anger do not sin": Do not let the
sun go down while you are still angry.*

EPHESIANS 4:26

*I*t's normal for your teens to get angry. Their anger is really just their expressing that they want something different for their lives and don't know how to make it happen. As Scripture says, "In your anger do not sin." In other words, they can be angry, but don't let your teen destroy themselves and the relationships around them because they don't know how to meet their own needs. That's where you come in. You are able to help them learn how to control their anger and let it motivate them to move on to bigger and better things.

Don't let their anger cause you to get angry. Let it move you to help your teen mature and control their emotions.

Indeed, there is no one on earth who is righteous,
no one who does what is right and never sins.

ECCLESIASTES 7:20

When you die and are gone, I hope that no one has the opportunity to share untold secrets and hidden parts of your life that will only taint your legacy and the image that your children have of you. When you admit your mistakes, your faults, and your blunders, you are not only showing those around you that you are human but are also giving them the chance to admit their wrongdoings and mistakes without shame.

No one is perfect. And when you create an atmosphere that allows imperfection, you are giving permission to your teen to talk about the reality of life, and you usher in genuineness and authenticity—two things your teen is earnestly searching for.

No one should seek their own
good, but the good of others.

1 CORINTHIANS 10:24

Arguments happen because we all think and feel differently. But they are not the end of a relationship, either with your spouse or your child. Arguments have an amazing way of showing us what our teen needs, and they expose our child's desire. A conflict is your opportunity to determine whether your teen is just being selfish or is really exposing a true need in their life.

It's okay to disagree. The challenge is to disagree and maintain the boundaries and rules you have established for your home and keep the relationship you have with your teen. Don't let an argument ruin a relationship that God has placed in your life.

*"Come to me, all you who are weary and
burdened, and I will give you rest."*

MATTHEW 11:28

Today's teen culture is quite contrary to many of the values and biblical principles that we want to build into the life of our children. The pressure builds not only with parents but also in the life of their child. And your teen will find a way to relieve that pressure. Whether that is in healthy or unhealthy ways, they want relief just as much as you do.

Start by sitting down and having discussions about reducing the stress in your home so that it can become a place of relief and rest. Change up some old expectations and lighten up on just a couple of rules. Small changes can have some amazingly huge effects.

*Finally, brothers and sisters, whatever is
true, whatever is noble, whatever is right,
whatever is pure, whatever is lovely, whatever
is admirable—if anything is excellent or
praiseworthy—think about such things.*

PHILIPPIANS 4:8

*P*erspective—it's not only what your grandkids want,
it's what they must have to balance the bombardment
of details and confusion that is raining on their life. Your
role is not to correct, to teach, or to take over a parent's
role but rather to give perspective to what happens in life,
helping your grandkids gain a greater understanding of
what's going on around them and what is truly important
as they move through adolescence.

Your place is to give a new angle, a new view, and a new
assessment on what is happening in their life. Don't share
what they already know; share what God has taught you in
the process of walking through life and understanding what
is truly important.

I do not understand what I do. For what I
want to do I do not do, but what I hate I do.
ROMANS 7:15

Your teen will have a great tendency to find themselves doing things they don't want to do and not doing the things that they really want to do. It's called human nature. They'll make mistakes, disappoint you, violate your rules, sneak around behind your back, and not listen to your sage advice, no matter how great it might be. They do so because they're adolescents in pursuit of independence, control, and the authority to make their own decisions.

Keep asking questions, and don't ever think that your teen will never make a mistake. They will. Understanding your role to pursue truth and grace in your parenting will draw your family closer together, even when your child goes behind your back.

Whoever heeds discipline shows the way to life, but
whoever ignores correction leads others astray.

PROVERBS 10:17

Rules without relationship causes rebellion. But relationship without rules causes chaos. Structure is needed if you want to create a home that controls selfishness and entitlement and moves a teen along a path that they can see is beneficial to them. In other words, they actually like having rules because it helps them.

Your teens desire structure. They want direction and guidance, and rules keep them on that path. Your goal should be to develop rules that can be embraced by all, are easy to follow, are easier to understand, and are always in the best interest of your teen. Start by coming up with five rules that would change the direction of your family and sticking with them, allowing consequences to have their full effect. Rules are needed, but relationship is the most important thing.

> *"The LORD bless you and keep you; the*
> *LORD make his face shine on you and*
> *be gracious to you; the LORD turn his*
> *face toward you and give you peace."*
>
> NUMBERS 6:24–26

Sadly, your teens aren't experiencing relationships at the level we did when we were their age. Social engagement in their world has changed with the introduction of texting and social networking sites. As a result, it is our purpose to give them a taste of what true relationships are while balancing their need for us to remain as the parent of the family.

Your role is to give them a taste of the character of God through your relationship with them. Their struggle to connect is our opportunity to engage in ways that our parents never did with us. You must be intentional in pursuing a relationship with your teens, just as God has pursued a relationship with you.

*For the Spirit God gave us does not make us
timid, but gives us power, love and self-discipline.*

2 TIMOTHY 1:7

I am thankful that your teen is attracted to someone of the opposite sex. It means that they are normal and that their God-given desires to one day choose a lifelong mate are being expressed as they find out more about how to engage with the opposite sex.

You have a choice here. You can live in fear of what might happen and try to prevent it. Or you can trust what you have taught your children in hopes that dating will be a training ground during their adolescent years. God has not given you a spirit of fear but of power, love, and a sound mind, so use all three when determining what is appropriate for your teen. They'll love your involvement in their lives.

*Do not be anxious about anything, but in
every situation, by prayer and petition, with
thanksgiving, present your requests to God.*

PHILIPPIANS 4:6

One of the hardest goals of parenting is to help our teens step away from us and step out on their own. Let me assure you, it doesn't mean that your parenting role is over; it's just going to change gears.

Many times, parents like to hang on to their kids, never letting them grow up and learn to live life without a dependence on mom and dad. But it is essential that we help train them to get to the point in life where they are not dependent on us. It makes for healthier marriages and allows you to become better parents. The result? You'll enjoy your kids as independents as much as you did when they were dependent on you. I promise.

Let your gentleness be evident
to all. The Lord is near.
PHILIPPIANS 4:5

Your teens are surrounded by negativity that focuses on who they aren't and what they'll never be or have and shames them for attempting to stand up for themselves or others. So many kids are more concerned about videoing negative behavior than they are about standing up to others to be a positive influence. It's a tough world.

Don't make it tougher for them. Your home needs to be a respite, a retreat from the pressures of life, where your kids know of your unfailing love for them. So quit correcting all the time, and stop pointing out all the insignificant aspects of their life. Let your praises be many and your criticisms be few. You are to be the same refuge for your kids that God is to you.

Where there is strife, there is pride, but
wisdom is found in those who take advice.
PROVERBS 13:10

The relationship you have with your teen now will determine the type of relationship you will have with your kids, and grandkids, ten years from now. Unresolved issues only arise at a later time in life when the consequences are greater and the rippling impact affects more people. Start doing what it takes to make sure that all issues are discussed, and work hard to maintain a relationship with your teen, even in the most uncomfortable of situations.

Your relationship with your teen is the most important relationship in their life. My prayer for you is that you will pursue resolution and your teen will be open to restoration. They want it; they just might not know how to do that. But they'll follow your lead.

And over all these virtues put on love, which
binds them all together in perfect unity.
COLOSSIANS 3:14

C hange happens, and it's happening quicker than any of us could ever imagine. The DNA of your kid's social structure will change a number of times before they graduate from high school, forcing you to be ever mindful and ready to make shifts in your parenting style to accommodate the changing needs of your teen.

You can change your style while keeping your same standards and emphases. This allows you to continue having an effective and up-to-date approach that will continue to help your teen walk in a manner that is worthy of the Lord. It's essential to let go of some ineffective ways of parenting and embrace those that will keep you connected to the ones you love dearly.

Whoever disregards discipline comes to poverty and
shame, but whoever heeds correction is honored.

PROVERBS 13:18

Your involvement in the life of your teen is paramount to the healthiness of your family. And I'm convinced that how you are involved will determine the depth of your relationship with your child in their adult years.

Make sure that you are working hard to maintain the relationship you have with your teen. And the crucial piece of that challenge is to create a relational atmosphere, structured by rules and boundaries, which guarantee a path that will lead your teen to success. And don't be afraid to deal with the real issues in your child's life. Resolve what needs to be solved so that problems aren't carried to the next generation.

Whoever sows to please their flesh, from the flesh
will reap destruction; whoever sows to please
the Spirit, from the Spirit will reap eternal life.

GALATIANS 6:8

Your ability to accommodate your parenting style to the needs of your teens will determine whether you are a success or a total failure in training up your teen to face the world as they know it. God has placed you in the life of your child for a reason: to teach them the values and principles that you hold dear to your heart and to encourage them to hold them just as dearly.

Shifting your emphasis from a teaching to a training model helps you change your approach as your teen matures and becomes a godly man or woman. The key is to engage in such a way that brings hope and helps them apply those values you have built into their life.

*"For if you forgive other people when they sin
against you, your heavenly Father will also
forgive you. But if you do not forgive others their
sins, your Father will not forgive your sins."*

MATTHEW 6:14–15

People ask me all the time how I live with teens who are constantly violating expectations and engaging in inappropriate behavior. I tell them this: you must love your teen more than you hate their behavior. Don't determine your love for your child by whether their behavior is acceptable or unacceptable. Love them because of who they are, not what they do.

I'm not saying that you should ignore their inappropriate behavior. You can't do that. But you must move toward them at a time when their behavior is pushing you away. It's called grace—loving them the same way that God loves you. It's not always easy, but it *is* essential to having a long-lasting relationship with your child.

Be very careful, then, how you live—not as unwise
but as wise, making the most of every opportunity.

EPHESIANS 5:15–16

Your teen is screaming for opportunities to gather wisdom, and their world of influence is coming up short, so your role is to be more than just a source of information. You must be someone who shares and displays wisdom. They will gather it the same way you gained yours: by learning from what you see, what you think about, and what you experience.

What wisdom do they collect as they observe you? Have you been giving insight through questions and discussions that go beyond scratching the surface? What experiences are you providing for them that display how to live wisely and impress on them the importance of turning from foolishness? You will be the most reliable and important source of wisdom for your teen, so be wise—they are watching your every move!

*Whatever you have learned or received or heard
from me, or seen in me—put it into practice.
And the God of peace will be with you.*

PHILIPPIANS 4:9

I can't say it enough: you are the most important relationship your teen will have. As they get busier and the
demands on them increase, you must work even harder to
ensure your place in their life. If you're like me, it's easy to
get busy—so busy that one day you'll ask, "Where did the
time go?"

If you don't spend the time with your teen, it will pass
before your eyes, and you'll one day regret not pouring
more of your life into theirs. If you don't do it, someone
else will. And your teen will never get from someone else
what they can get from you alone. God has placed you in
their life for a reason, and that reason can only be found in
a relationship.

*But as for you, be strong and do not give
up, for your work will be rewarded.*

2 CHRONICLES 15:7

Your teens want to talk. They just don't know how because the culture of their generation is more about communicating with their thumbs than with their mouths. They live in a world where it's more about presentation than content, more about appearance than the condition of the heart.

You haven't been replaced; you've been nudged out— not by a generation gap but by a technological influence that thrives on appearance and presentation. Your teens likely aren't ignoring you intentionally; they're just consumed by the norms of their society. Your role is to break through this cultural influence and give them a taste of what deep and meaningful conversation is all about. You'll have to be intentional if you want to be more effective than what they learn from their phone.

*But the Lord is faithful, and he will
strengthen you and protect you.*

2 THESSALONIANS 3:3

I've never met a set of parents that wants to be in control
of their adult child, but I've known quite a few that have
kids in their twenties who have no control over their lives.
A parent's well-founded intent to provide can quickly move
into enabling. So quit enabling and start equipping!

I want you to hear this: a bumpy transition into adulthood is usually the fault of parents who won't relinquish
control of their child's life. It's time to start planning how
you will give a little more control to your teen through their
adolescent years. They want it, so give it to them. And be
present in their life to help them learn how to take control.

*Keep me as the apple of your eye; hide
me in the shadow of your wings.*

PSALM 17:8

*D*o you remember a summer in your high school years that was fun and relaxing? Do you remember how those lazy days gave you a sense of refreshment and encouragement when the pressures of school and your social world were just a little overwhelming? Well, your teens want that same experience.

I would encourage you to make this coming summer a season of relationship, a time where you and your teen can re-establish the relationship you've always had. This will reassure your child that no matter how intense a school year can be, both academically and socially, there will always be a place of fun and relationship in your home. Make this summer one that is magnificent, meaningful, and memorable.

*Even youths grow tired and weary, and young
men stumble and fall; but those who hope in
the LORD will renew their strength. They will
soar on wings like eagles; they will run and not
grow weary, they will walk and not be faint.*

ISAIAH 40:30–31

Given time, your kids will wound your heart in one way or another. Their words, actions, or decisions will eventually cause pain in your life. It's inevitable. But you know what? It's not about you. God placed you in your child's life to be a reflection of His love. He wants you to be His Word becoming flesh in your teen's life so that they will get a taste of His character at the time of their greatest need.

It's not always easy, but it is rewarding over time. Don't let your own hurt keep you from helping the one hurting in your family. God will help you get through your struggles, just as you help your teen get through theirs.

He is before all things, and in him
all things hold together.

COLOSSIANS 1:17

Many times, moms and dads wonder where they went wrong and what they missed in their teen's life, as if they are the cause of the particular struggle their teen is going through.

At times like these, it is important to remember that as culture changes, God does not. The struggle for many parents is learning new ways of adapting timeless truth to a world that seems to be working against parents and grandparents.

If your teen falls into one of those traps and end up somewhere you had hoped they wouldn't be, the greatest truth your child needs is that, while you may not agree with their behavior, you will always love them regardless of their choices, just as God loves us.

Therefore we do not lose heart. Though outwardly we are wasting away, yet inwardly we are being renewed day by day. For our light and momentary troubles are achieving for us an eternal glory that far outweighs them all.

2 CORINTHIANS 4:16–17

I want you to know that God is keeping you around so that you can have an influence on your grandchildren. They need to receive from you the wisdom and perspective they can get from no one else. The greatest challenge that all grandparents have is remaining engaged and influential in the life of their teen grandchild. You must shift your way of engaging as their needs change, and to do this you must remain connected. Change as they change. Don't talk about your medical problems. Don't be judgmental. And stop complaining about everything. Provide a place of rest, one where your grandkids will know of your unconditional love and constant encouragement.

A good person leaves an inheritance for
their children's children, but a sinner's
wealth is stored up for the righteous.

PROVERBS 13:22

You don't have to save the best for last—the best is the time that you have today. Your grandkids need you to be a messenger of timeless truth in their ever-changing world. Trust me when I say that they need you a lot more than you need them.

Proverbs says, "A good person leaves an inheritance for their children's children." The legacy you leave as an inheritance is not just about what you've left in their bank account; it's measured by what you've deposited in their heart. Help them see the world through eyes that have had wonderful experiences and have seen more than they have. Give them perspective on life. It's that big-picture view that helps you see more than what is physically evident and beyond what is right before you.

We have confidence in the Lord that you are doing
and will continue to do the things we command.

2 THESSALONIANS 3:4

Your teens need you desperately. They need your genuine and authentic lifestyle that displays the values and biblical insights you've gathered through your years. So it's important for them to see the value of a connection with you and for you to value them as they mature and learn to spread their wings. I'm sure that, if you're like me, you don't want their preteen years to be your greatest memories of your relationship with your kids. You want your relationship to continue to grow as they do, and you want to maintain and deepen your relationship in the days ahead. To do that, you've got to know their needs and strive to meet theirs, just as God meets yours.

But you, LORD, are a shield around me, my glory, the One who lifts my head high.

PSALM 3:3

I don't think I will ever understand why someone would want to cut their life short. That's because I have never been in that dark place. But I have seen many people from all walks of life with all sorts of issues take their life. And I have spent countless hours with families who spend years trying to process that which just can't be. All the families I know who have lost their kids never saw it coming. And most never had the discussion with their teen about how painful life would be without them in it. So what is a parent to do? Have discussions and talk about the dark feelings your teen may occasionally feel, and let them know of the blessing they are to your family.

The LORD is compassionate and gracious,
slow to anger, abounding in love.

PSALM 103:8

When raising teens, conflict is inevitable. And just because you don't ever see it doesn't mean it's not there. Make an effort to provide the setting and let your teen know that there is nothing you won't talk about and no topic that you'll ignore when it comes to healthiness of your family.

If you want to love the way Christ loves you, run toward your child when everything is telling you to run the other way. It's called grace—moving toward your daughter when everything she is doing is pushing you away, or extending the hand of kindness to your son when he's violated your cherished principles.

Conflict is a precursor to change, and change is how one matures and grows. Avoiding areas of conflict prevents you and your teen from experiencing the grace of God manifested in your presence.

Those who disregard discipline despise
themselves, but the one who heeds
correction gains understanding.

PROVERBS 15:32

*I*t might not seem like it sometimes, but your teen wants structure and boundaries. They long for clarity of what is okay and what is off limits. Just as man plans and God directs his path, do the same for your teen. Let your son or daughter make decisions about how they'll walk on the path you have set before them.

And don't rescue your teen from the consequences that come with making poor decisions and unwise choices. God will use these to teach your child the difference between right and wrong and will help them understand the need to wisely think through their decision-making process. Your boundaries will help them mature and develop into healthy young adults.

*Show proper respect to everyone, love
the family of believers, fear God.*

1 PETER 2:17

Respect is probably the most important value within your home, and it must be conveyed by actions and communicated by words. Initially, it begins with the example you set before your children, then it develops into opportunities to show respect amid conflict and difficulties. Respect is the one essential element that sets the stage for all other aspects of interaction within your home.

Disrespect destroys relationships. If you have been disrespectful to your teens, then admit your attitude and begin a new path that is based on respect of everyone. Your kids will one day thank you for your example and the requirements you made of each family member.

And as for you, brothers and sisters,
never tire of doing what is good.

2 THESSALONIANS 3:13

It is easy to become battle weary and sometimes lose perspective on the deep relationships that have been developed in your family. If you find this happening in your home, you must take some time to reinforce the relationships in the family and deal with the problems before you head on.

Most of these issues are temporary and will soon pass, so know that you are going to get to the other side of the conflict you now face. God has promised that the challenges are momentary and will soon be in your rearview mirror. So hang on to the relationships within your family and to the promises that God shares with us. He will one day take all your trials and sorrows and turn them into something beautiful.

*Therefore each of you must put off falsehood
and speak truthfully to your neighbor, for
we are all members of one body.*

EPHESIANS 4:25

A teen who cannot be truthful with you only compounds the problems you face, and that which cannot be corrected now will only bring greater consequences in the future. It is just like a bad habit that will grow worse if ignored. It's essential that you tackle the issue now and fight the good fight that has been placed before you.

One principle in training horses is to ask first, then demand. With your teen, ask that the lying be addressed, then demand that the lying stop. Be clear that you want the truth, the whole truth, and nothing but the truth. Set the example to the one who has a problem with lying. Live a life full of grace and truth.

> *For the grace of God has appeared that*
> *offers salvation to all people. It teaches us*
> *to say "No" to ungodliness and worldly*
> *passions, and to live self-controlled, upright*
> *and godly lives in this present age.*

TITUS 2:11–12

A teen's character is the fruit of the seeds that have been sown into their life. When your child reaches adolescence, it's an opportunity for them to flesh out the important biblical truths and moral standards you have taught them. And it's a time of training a child how to apply what he or she knows to be true in relationships and situations in their life.

Your teen's character will flow from the new person that Christ has made them to be. It will be heard in their speech and actions that flow from the abundance of what has been placed in their heart. This is where the Christian life is more caught than taught, so give them an example to follow and encourage them to take life-changing words and put them into action.

The LORD is my shepherd, I lack nothing.
He makes me lie down in green pastures, he leads
me beside quiet waters, he refreshes my soul.

PSALM 23:1–3

Your teen needs a place of rest, a respite, somewhere they can be refreshed and be ready for another day of challenges from a culture we've all been grateful we didn't have to grow up in.

They need a break from the intensity of a culture that is all about appearance and performance. If you're performance oriented and are big on appearance, make sure that your expectations aren't setting your teen up for failure. This means reflecting on what you are wanting from your teens and making sure you're giving them enough down time to learn how to relax, renew, and refresh. It will change the way your family members relate to one another.

Surely your goodness and love will follow
me all the days of my life, and I will dwell
in the house of the LORD forever.

PSALM 23:6

Just because your teen is losing interest in church does not mean they no longer have a love for Christ. Either the busyness of their life is putting their relationship on hold or they aren't having their needs met, so they're looking for solutions to their life issues elsewhere.

Whatever the reason, it's important for your teen to know that you can love them whether they go to church or not. That will also remove from them the opportunity to use their church attendance as a challenge mechanism to show you that they are in control of their life.

Let them make some decisions, and let their faith be "theirs." God has promised that what has been sown into their life will one day come to fruition. That's a promise you can trust!

Whoever is patient has great understanding,
but one who is quick-tempered displays folly.

PROVERBS 14:29

Scripture tells us, "be angry, but don't sin." Your teen needs to know when they've crossed that line. But don't write off all their anger as selfishness or rebellion; it may be a sign that, in all their attempts to make life work, they're not having their needs met.

And when Scripture tells you to not let the sun go down on your anger, the encouragement is to not ignore what you're wanting from your teens as well.

When anger reveals itself, it means there's a need to find out what expectation is not being met and to have a good discussion about how you can meet the needs of your teens.

Be strong and courageous.
Do not be afraid or terrified because of them,
for the LORD your God goes with you; he
will never leave you nor forsake you.

DEUTERONOMY 31:6

Teens need privacy. It's easy to give it to them when they're doing everything correctly and in a respectful way. Just because they make some mistakes along the way—which will happen because they're adolescents—doesn't mean you have to take away their privacy. It means you must help instill a greater sense of responsibility in their life.

Putting in the effort to maintain an open and thriving relationship means you must work to keep communication lines open. That just doesn't happen on its own. Your investigations and excessive worrying will only damage your relationship, but your pursuit of connecting will eliminate your desire to snoop and pry into the privacy of your teen.

His divine power has given us everything we need
for a godly life through our knowledge of him
who called us by his own glory and goodness.

2 PETER 1:3

*P*art of parenting demands that you protect your kids from their foolish thinking and damaging decisions, all while training them to become independent and learn about choices and consequences. It's a delicate balance, but one that is necessary if you're going to raise healthy teens who know how to make wise decisions in a danger-filled culture.

Do you know how you do that? You ask. You ask God for wisdom. You ask your teens what they think. And you ask your friends for counsel and insight. God does work all things together for good.

Remember this: He uses pain to create passion and purpose. He makes your mess into your message. He takes tests and turns them into testimonies.

Do not conform to the pattern of this world, but be
transformed by the renewing of your mind. Then
you will be able to test and approve what God's
will is—his good, pleasing and perfect will.

ROMANS 12:2

As your teens get older and older, let them flex their decision-making muscles. It's the only way those muscles are going to get stronger. It's much more important for your teen to develop discernment and learn to make wise choices than it is for you to be in control and protect them from risks. Let them decide, even when you don't think they'll choose correctly, and give them the opportunity to figure things out without fear of ridicule and shame.

Your presence in their life while they're making decisions will give you the opportunity to have some influence and give input before they leave home and have to make those decisions on their own.

*May the God who gives endurance and
encouragement give you the same attitude of
mind toward each other that Christ Jesus had.*

ROMANS 15:5

You have an amazing opportunity to leave a legacy of hope in your grandkids' lives in a way no one else can. A legacy is measured not by what you leave in their bank account but by what you have deposited in their hearts. God is keeping you around longer so you can leave a legacy that will change the direction of your teen grandkids' lives and influence their choices for the rest of their lives.

Determine how you can be a source of encouragement and how to give perspective to a generation that desperately wants (and greatly needs) the wisdom and insight you possess.

I can do all this through him who gives me strength.

PHILIPPIANS 4:13

If you're the parent of an adopted child, your efforts and commitment to the expansion of your family are to be applauded and celebrated, whether it's going well or you're struggling through the adolescent years. I want you to remember this: when your adopted child reaches their teens, a time when they are longing to belong, there is a great possibility that they will wonder why they were abandoned and given up.

Listen well and know that the answers you gave in their earlier years won't work during their adolescent years. Their way of thinking has changed, and so must your approach to giving them the answers they long to hear. Don't give up. You are to be applauded and celebrated for your commitment to your adopted child.

*Being confident of this, that he who began
a good work in you will carry it on to
completion until the day of Christ Jesus.*

PHILIPPIANS 1:6

God bless those who choose to give a child a new home and a new family. If you are adoptive parents, may your home be a haven of hope for a child who needs you, may God's beautiful provision for orphans reach down to you as well, and may He give you the strength to work through any future struggles or difficulties.

The challenges you face during the adolescent years with your adopted teen are preparing them for a full life knowing that they are loved and belong to your family. Whatever you face with your adopted teen today will soon pass as they mature and understand the sacrifice you have endured for their sake.

All hard work brings a profit, but
mere talk leads only to poverty.

PROVERBS 14:23

Our kids live in a world of entitlement that teaches them to take for granted all that they have and to constantly desire more. It's a part of their culture. They're being shaped that way, and it is your responsibility to cultivate thankfulness and gratitude in your teens, which are attributes that come from an understanding that they are owed nothing. The older they get, the less dependent they should be on you for the accumulation of money and possessions. Once they are made to work for what they have, their gratitude for those items or services provided for them will be greatly appreciated.

So then, just as you received Christ Jesus as Lord,
continue to live your lives in him, rooted and
built up in him, strengthened in the faith as you
were taught, and overflowing with thankfulness.

COLOSSIANS 2:6–7

The desire to control your kid's life comes easily. It's rooted in your attempt to protect them from the world's influence and to keep them on the right path so they may walk in a manner worthy of the Lord. And it works—when your child is younger. But once they reach twelve or thirteen, they want to take control and start making decisions. So let them! Give them more and more privileges and responsibilities as they age so they can be trained how to make wise decisions in a foolish world. Loosen your grip on their privileges so they'll appreciate your involvement in their life as you help them mature and grow into responsible adults.

Even fools are thought wise if they keep silent,
and discerning if they hold their tongues.

PROVERBS 17:28

There's an old proverb that says, "A fool speaks; the wise man listens!" Another says, "A fool appears wise when he keeps his mouth shut." And yet another states, "A fool delights in sharing his opinion." Get the message? The point is to encourage all of us to hear what our teens are saying and to grasp the message of their heart so we may respond in a wise and appropriate way. A smart parent believes only half of what he or she hears; a wise parent knows which half.

Your teens are craving a listening ear in hopes of having someone understand who they are. My prayer is that you'll understand that God gave you two ears and one mouth because He wants you to listen twice as much as you speak.

I press on toward the goal to win the prize for which
God has called me heavenward in Christ Jesus.

PHILIPPIANS 3:14

Some of your old ways of parenting were magnificent in their day. Your kids listened, they obeyed, they followed, and they respected the position you held in their life. But some of those old ways just do not work anymore, and you must shift your parenting style to accommodate the needs of your teen to bring timeless truth to their ever-changing culture. You must shift your style to make sure that your teen continues to view you as they did in the younger years: as one who loves them dearly, will offer help when needed, and will not be distracted in helping them become the person God has created them to be.

Her children arise and call her blessed; her
husband also, and he praises her: "Many women
do noble things, but you surpass them all."
PROVERBS 31:28–29

Moms, there are very few people who can do what you do. You love in ways that are mind boggling to the other half of the population. You stand by your children when everyone else wants to walk away. You believe the best about your loved ones and never miss a birthday, an anniversary, or an opportunity to spend more and more time with other parts of the family.

You are a wealth of wisdom, and men know it. You have the power to speak truth into the lives of your kids in a way no one else can. Your children and grandchildren listen to you more than anyone else. You pray in a way that touches the heart of God and influences the lives of those around you. Don't let anyone think less of the mighty woman you are. You are blessed, and those around you praise you for all that you do.

From everyone who has been given much, much
will be demanded; and from the one who has been
entrusted with much, much more will be asked.

LUKE 12:48

*I*t bears repeating for the sake of your teens: find time to spend with them. And in that, you'll find that they'll cherish your love more and more, which opens the door for them to respond to responsibilities you give them. Give them more and more and require more and more from them.

This will produce a healthier relationship and teach them a great truth in life that wise living produces happiness, that foolishness brings pain, and that they must be mature and trustworthy with what they've been given.

As you give, ask that they do the same. Give more freedom, more independence, and more opportunity to make decisions, and do so with the hope of their response leading them to maturity.

*"A good man brings good things out of the good
stored up in his heart, and an evil man brings
evil things out of the evil stored up in his heart.
For the mouth speaks what the heart is full of."*

LUKE 6:45

The tendency most of us have is to attempt to control our teen when we feel their behavior is inappropriate or out of control. When they are making poor choices that could affect them for the rest of their life, it's important that we provide external boundaries where internal boundaries don't exist. But it's equally important that we deal with the deep heart issues that show up through their behavior. Get to the heart of the issue, deal with the root cause, and resolve issues during adolescence so they don't arise later in life when the consequences will be greater and affect more people. As the old saying goes, there's no time like the present.

*So I reflected on all this and concluded
that the righteous and the wise and
what they do are in God's hands.*

ECCLESIASTES 9:1

*F*orgiveness is sometimes hard. But it's a more difficult position to pray to be more Christlike and yet
not forgive someone. For to be like Him is to be quick
to forgive. Everything that has happened to you has first
passed through the hands of God. He uses the events of
your life to transform you more into His image. Your future
is too precious to hold on to hurts and grudges that will
only drag you down and keep you from loving the way that
God has loved you.

How about it? Is it time to make that call and move
toward the one you have every reason to walk away from?
That's called grace, and you will never be more like Christ
than when you offer it to that certain person in your life
who has offended you.

Who is wise and understanding among you?
Let them show it by their good life, by deeds
done in the humility that comes from wisdom.

JAMES 3:13

D o you ever wonder if your teen is having trouble thinking through decisions and coming to wise conclusions? Are you the one keeping them from learning how to search for the greater good and the better conclusions? Do you think it's time for them to learn how to search rather than always being given the easy answer? Does your teen feel valued when you ask them a question? Does it show that you are interested in what they think? Do your questions show interest in hearing what's on their mind? Do you think that your example of asking questions shows them how to do the same? Isn't now a good time to quit giving answers and start asking questions?

*"Take my yoke upon you and learn from
me, for I am gentle and humble in heart,
and you will find rest for your souls."*

MATTHEW 11:29

Jesus said, "Come to me, all you who are weary and burdened, and I will give you rest." What a great challenge for each of us as parents and grandparents to provide that place for our children who are sometimes battle weary from the tough and confusing culture they are growing up in.

You create the atmosphere at home. You create that safe harbor for a teen who is going through the storms of life. So how about it? Is your home sterile? Is it one where everyone walks on eggshells? Or is it one that welcomes the overwhelmed teen trying to survive their adolescent years?

Do not forsake wisdom, and she will protect you;
love her, and she will watch over you.

PROVERBS 4:6

You've heard me say it before: if you have a discipline problem, you have a relationship problem. If you're winning the battles but losing the war going on in everyday life, then I doubt you're loving your child as God loves you. Be wise: pick your battles. Determine which hill is worth dying on. And realize that you can't correct everything, so pick the strategy where you may lose a few battles but hopefully win the war.

Balance your words of correction with actions of encouragement, inspiration, praise, and support so that your teen knows that you are not "on them" but are "for them." Be wise and strategic and ask your teen how he or she thinks you can love them more.

MAY 17

I myself am convinced, my brothers and sisters,
that you yourselves are full of goodness, filled with
knowledge and competent to instruct one another.

ROMANS 15:14

The most important relationship your child will have during their adolescent years is the one they have with you! You will be the one who offers encouragement, instills values, and helps them develop the skills needed to make it in life. It all happens because of the kind of relationship that doesn't walk away from them if they are lost, doesn't leave if they make poor choices, and always offers a hug of grace when it's needed most. Your teen needs you. I've never met a teen who doesn't long for a good relationship with their parents. So what are you doing to make that relationship happen? You are the one who creates the atmosphere of relationship and possibility for change.

May the Lord direct your hearts into
God's love and Christ's perseverance.

2 THESSALONIANS 3:5

Bullying has been around since the beginning of mankind. But the level we currently see it at and the way society currently allows it are unique. Social networking has changed the face of the bully and given them the power to change the direction of your teen's life with just a few texts or messages. It's important that you keep your finger on the pulse of your child's social life and keep a close eye on any behavior changes that might indicate they're being bullied or put into situations they never wanted to be in. Your teen needs your help and protection.

Neither height nor depth, nor anything else in
all creation, will be able to separate us from the
love of God that is in Christ Jesus our Lord.

ROMANS 8:39

It's vital that a teen hears that they are still loved when they make a poor choice and are suffering the consequences of their decision. Moms and dads, your teen needs to know that you love them when all is well and when all is not so good. Genuine love remains, regardless of performance or poor choices. Let consequences have their full effect, but don't shame a child because they made a mistake. All teens make mistakes—just as you did. What they need is the hug of grace and the encouragement of the ones who instilled a sense of value in their life: you! Never does the love of a mom or dad show itself more than when a child knows of a parent's never-ending and unfailing love.

Therefore if you have any encouragement from being united with Christ, if any comfort from his love, if any common sharing in the Spirit, if any tenderness and compassion, then make my joy complete by being like-minded, having the same love, being one in spirit and of one mind.

PHILIPPIANS 2:1–2

I doubt that many parents understand the crucial role their relationship plays in the success of their child's adolescent years. Your teen needs you and is looking to you to provide what only a parent can deliver: the structure that keeps a teen on track, a relationship where nothing a child does can diminish a parent's love, and a communication style that invites discussion and always provides a listening ear.

These are tough times for kids. They're also scary times for parents, who never know when their teen will stumble and fall into the dark hole of confusion. There are some things you can do to fulfill what your teen is hoping for. Give it a shot. Try something different. What you do in these years will determine the type of relationship you have with your teen in the next chapter of your child's life.

For through wisdom your days will be many, and
years will be added to your life.
If you are wise, your wisdom will reward you.
PROVERBS 9:11–12

*I*f you are doing a good job at parenting, there will still be some tense times that arise when you least expect it. And if you're wise, you'll do some things to calm the situation and allow the emotions to mellow. Counter the first response with a better one that will calm emotions, affirm relationship, and let your teen know that your relationship can and will survive any storm or conflict that comes your way.

Create an atmosphere that allows your teen to rest in your home. Encourage your teen to work through any crisis with you rather than fight against you. You set the tone for your home, so work hard to get it right and create an environment that cultivates relationship with your teen.

*Taste and see that the LORD is good; blessed
is the one who takes refuge in him.*

PSALM 34:8

No one goes through life without experiencing difficulties, hardships, losses, or times when something
important gets taken away or hopes and dreams get dashed,
leaving one feeling somewhat empty and disappointed in
the way life is turning out. Your teen is no exception.

The wise parent does a couple of things. First, learn
about your own losses and how those have motivated your
behavior. Second, look for losses in your teen's life that are
motivating their behavior. That's how you get to the heart
of the issue and see real change in conduct and attitudes.

Loss can play a huge part in the life of your teen, even
when they don't realize the emptiness they are trying to fill.
But no loss is so big that God can't fill it.

Let the peace of Christ rule in your hearts,
since as members of one body you were
called to peace. And be thankful.

COLOSSIANS 3:15

We are "pioneer" parents and grandparents. We're all trying to figure out how to balance the new tools of technology with our family traditions, values, and priorities. Ignoring the new ways our teens engage and socialize doesn't solve the challenge of helping them find a balance between developing their relationships and using the tools of technology.

We must encourage relationships, place age-appropriate boundaries where needed, and show our teens a balanced life—which means our lives are not being consumed by technology as well. As you help your teens, determine a balance for your own tech life. We are pioneering through advances that can either enhance or ruin relationships. Set some boundaries, have good conversations, and don't let entertainment overtake the value you bring to your child's life.

*We ought always to thank God for you,
brothers and sisters, and rightly so, because your
faith is growing more and more, and the love
all of you have for one another is increasing.*

2 THESSALONIANS 1:3

When your child reaches their teen years, it's important for you to shift your parenting style to accommodate the new needs of your adolescent who desires to take more control of their life, make more decisions, become more independent, have more discussions, and learn how to apply all you've taught them.

Many times, a parent's intent to help only provokes resentment, especially with older teens who really do want to grow up and take responsibility for their life. Quit being so strict. Give your teen some room to make mistakes. I promise they'll learn from poor choices—just as you did when you were their age. Don't provoke your child to wrath with overcontrolling restrictions, but teach them to accept responsibility (something they'll need in the future), knowing that maturity can come no other way.

"Let not the wise boast of their wisdom or the strong boast of their strength or the rich boast of their riches, but let the one who boasts boast about this: that they have the understanding to know me, that I am the LORD, who exercises kindness, justice and righteousness on earth, for in these I delight."

JEREMIAH 9:23–24

I sometimes wonder what our teens would say about what we as parents talk about the most. When all the joking is eliminated and all small talk comments about weather, sports, etc. along with all your opinions are taken away, what type of conversation do you have with your teens?

Try to eliminate some of the "fluff" in your conversations and get down to the deeper issues of your teen's life. Try to not talk about you as much and create "an ear" to pick up on clues and times that your teen welcomes your conversation. Ask yourself, "Do they know God better because they know me and see the example that I set before them?"

*Finally, be strong in the Lord
and in his mighty power.*

EPHESIANS 6:10

One of the greatest reasons parents have for not turning over control to their teen and allowing them to start making decisions about their life is the fear of losing their purpose in their child's life.

Let me assure you of something: some of the greatest joys you can experience as a parent are when you allow your child to take control of their own life. You then get to move into an even greater role of helping your child raise their own children. The parenting process just keeps getting better—but only if you release your grip so your child can take hold of their life. If you don't, they'll break away and never come back. So give up your control and know that God will use you in new and rewarding ways in the future days with your teen.

You are my hiding place; you will protect me from trouble and surround me with songs of deliverance.

PSALM 32:7

When your teen becomes quiet, you must know that something is going on. Maybe they don't know how to talk about deeper issues. Maybe they don't know the words that accurately express these new feelings they are experiencing. Or maybe something has happened that they don't know how to talk about.

Whatever the reason, your child's silence is screaming for your attention. So don't ignore the silent cries for help and engagement, the silent requests for your involvement in their life when they don't know how to ask for it, and the silent pleas for hope that can't be put into words.

Teens shut down for a reason, and it's your task to find out what that is. And that is never accomplished by you being silent.

Remember those earlier days.

HEBREWS 10:32

We all have a tendency to forget the past just a little too quickly, thus keeping us from reflecting on how the hand of God has been working in our lives all along. Remember the good times and the bad times. The weaving of the two, the blessings and the losses, will reveal a patchwork story of your life that is truly the handiwork of God.

It's amazing to me that we try to forget the painful moments in life when, in reality, those are the times we learned the most. We brush past our losses because of their discomfort, yet eventually we figure out that moving into uncomfortable areas of life gives us the wisdom to handle the harder tasks that lie ahead.

If everything that comes to us has first passed through the hands of God, then it is important to remember what we've been through so that we can allow those lessons to transform us more into His image. Remember those earlier days.

*We have this hope as an anchor for
the soul, firm and secure.*

HEBREWS 6:19

Whenever you see a change in your teen's behavior (especially when they begin to shut down and "give up"), nine times out of ten something has happened that caused them to lose hope that tomorrow will be any better.

Their "shut down" is a first sign of a change in their perception of their world. They might self-medicate, find a new set of friends, give up on some dreams they've held dear, and begin to feel distant from you.

The key is to keep communication lines open and determine if you are a cause of an overload that might be weighing them down. If you are, then change it up a bit and relieve the pressure that might be pushing them to the edge. Don't ignore the signs of a lack of motivation—it's a flashing light on the dashboard of your teen's life.

*The LORD will keep you from all harm—he will
watch over your life; the LORD will watch over
your coming and going both now and forevermore."*

PSALM 121:7–8

*I*t's a crazy and changing world, isn't it? Especially when your teen comes to you and expresses things that you never thought you would ever hear come out of their mouth. I'm not sure that I have all the answers to many changes we see in today's culture. But I do know this: your relationship with your child is just as important when they're making choices that clash with your values as when they are choosing in agreement with them.

The greatest commandment remains true—we must love one another, even when someone holds contrary beliefs or opposite viewpoints. All deserve compassion and love, and all are worthy of being treated with dignity and respect, even when a parent is discouraged by a teen's choice or position. We are to love others the way God loves us, and our child is no exception.

And God is able to bless you abundantly, so that
in all things at all times, having all that you
need, you will abound in every good work.

2 CORINTHIANS 9:8

Have you ever wanted to give up on your teen? Do you just want to throw in the towel because you're tired of being hurt, disappointed, and discouraged? Tired of having your heart broken? We've all been there; you're not alone.

To move toward your teen when you have every reason to walk away takes courage. It's called grace: offering relationship when it would be easier just to leave it alone. The latter never accomplishes anything except postponing the healing that needs to take place. Grace is essential so you can continue to be to your child who God has called you to be at a time when your child needs you the most.

Do not let any unwholesome talk come out
of your mouths, but only what is helpful
for building others up according to their
needs, that it may benefit those who listen.

EPHESIANS 4:29

Scripture reminds us that the words of the reckless pierce like swords, but the tongue of the wise brings healing. Proverbs also tells us that a fool vents anything he wants, but a wise man quietly holds back. There are plenty of things to complain about in this world, but our teens shouldn't be the focus of our complaining. They get enough of it in their own world.

My encouragement would be to spend more time *connecting* than *correcting*. Your relationship with your teen is the most important influence in their life. Don't ruin your opportunity to connect by indulging your desire to correct. Remember, the tongue of the wise brings healing.

Be very careful [that you are] ... making the most of every opportunity, because the days are evil.

EPHESIANS 5:15-16

Who would have ever thought that today's teen entertainment would entail a controller in hand while staring at a video screen? It's not a passing fad that entertains a few; it's now a staple of the adolescent culture that involves millions. One of our new jobs as a parent is to not only help them moderate the time they spend on this enticing attraction but also to help provide alternative activities that involve an opportunity for relationship—especially a relationship with you.

It might involve using your creativity to find an amusing activity you can do together or engaging in discussions and developing pastimes and hobbies that build enduring habits of involvement. We are the alternative to what our teen's culture is offering, so we must also use our time wisely.

Let us hold unswervingly to the hope we
profess, for he who promised is faithful.

HEBREWS 10:23

*I*n a culture where many teens feel that there is no hope of getting through their adolescent years, your child not only needs God to instill hope in their lives; they need you as well. The world in which they feel despondent is the same world where you must convey hope, encourage optimism, and restore confidence in God's plan for your teen's life to prosper. You can become the living expression of the Scriptures that you've hidden in your heart for years, and out of the abundance of your heart, your mouth will speak the wisdom and encouragement that God has given you.

JUNE 4

Set a guard over my mouth, LORD;
keep watch over the door of my lips.

PSALM 141:3

It's better to have a teen who expresses themselves than one who never speaks a word. It's a good thing to have kids share their thoughts and ideas. The challenge for us all is to help them do so in a way that encourages relationships with others and draws people together rather than creates divisiveness.

It's letting them know that even though you might disagree on some issues, you can still have a thriving and ever-growing relationship. Differences of opinions provide opportunities to learn, and viewpoints that don't see eye-to-eye are a wonderful occasion for going deeper in relationship. Differences make life exciting, and dissimilarities bring an attractive "seasoning" to life.

And it all begins with the way that you communicate and express relationship in your words.

Be wise in the way you act toward outsiders;
make the most of every opportunity.
Let your conversation be always full of
grace, seasoned with salt, so that you
may know how to answer everyone.

COLOSSIANS 4:5–6

The teens in your life are full of information but are starving for a connection with sources of wisdom. You are one of those sources! Wisdom is gained through observation, reflection, and experience. What wisdom have you gathered, and what knowledge and understanding do you possess that would benefit those teens? Your perceptions are important, and your hard-won lessons are vital to the development of minds that are filled with information but short on wisdom. Your challenge is to share that wisdom in a way that is seen as relevant to your teen and is not just forced on them as yet another lecture to endure.

*Now may the Lord of peace himself
give you peace at all times and in every
way. The Lord be with all of you.*

2 THESSALONIANS 3:16

You have so many opportunities to correct your teen that it's essential you figure out what is important to address and what is not. There are so many lessons to learn in life, but not all of them have to be learned during the adolescent years. And some of those lessons will be taught by others, at a different time, in a different place. Your challenge is to figure out which lessons your teen needs to learn from you right now and which can be left alone to be tackled later.

Don't die on a hill that will be soon be forgotten. Correct less and connect more, knowing that the example you set before your teen will have a greater impact than you will ever know.

Each one should test their own actions. Then
they can take pride in themselves alone, without
comparing themselves to someone else, for
each one should carry their own load.

GALATIANS 6:4–5

*I*t's amazing to me how teens begin to change once they are paid to do a job. They learn to listen to someone else, the value of a dollar, what it means to work rather than feeling entitled, and what it is to serve others. These lessons can be learned only by holding a job that gives them a taste of what their future life will be and gives them the encouragement to prepare themselves for the future.

Your teen can learn life lessons from someone other than you, and these experiences will validate and reinforce what you have been trying to teach them for years. Your son or daughter will one day thank you for pushing them to become financially responsible and break their sense of entitlement.

JUNE 8

"Give me wisdom and knowledge, that I may lead."

2 CHRONICLES 1:10

As the world becomes more permissive and the availability of marijuana and alcohol becomes more prevalent, it is important to convey an understanding of your teen's culture while also being ready and available to give guidance and direction. The most effective way of keeping a child from becoming dependent on any substance or activity is a relationship—the one your teen has with you.

Your genuine approach and authentic responses to the questions your teen poses about marijuana and alcohol will help them embrace the values and principles that you hold.

So do this: have open and frank discussions with your teen. Explain to them why you feel the way you do about alcohol and marijuana. Share your experiences. And share the wisdom you have gathered through your years of experience.

Let us not become weary in doing
good, for at the proper time we will
reap a harvest if we do not give up.
GALATIANS 6:9

Keep holding on, all you single moms. I'm convinced that if you continue to do what is right, your relationship with your teen will hold up as they age and further understand the difficult position you have been in.

Don't try to be the dad. Just keep being that caring mom who learns to establish some good boundaries and follows through on the consequences you've outlined. Don't let your occasional need to be tough blur the tenderness of the relationship you have with your kids. Be the mom God created you to be, and allow the losses of your child's life to be filled, in time, by God, who is close to the brokenhearted.

To bestow on them a crown of beauty instead
of ashes, the oil of joy instead of mourning,
and a garment of praise instead
of a spirit of despair.

ISAIAH 61:3

If you are a grandparent who is raising your grandkids because of a crisis in your family, I am sure the crisis you are experiencing is not exactly the hand you wanted dealt to you. But over time, with guidance and direction, hope will be renewed and relationships will be restored. This time for your family is but a passing moment. I am convinced that God will honor His promise to work all things—the good and the bad—for your good and His glory. Hold on to His promises and to the One who promises to never leave you or forsake you. With His help, you can make it through this.

For even when we were with you,
we gave you this rule: "The one who is
unwilling to work shall not eat."

2 THESSALONIANS 3:10

We all desire to see self-motivation develop within the life of our teen who has taken a backseat approach to life. We all hope that a child who is "just along for the ride" will soon begin walking their own path. Any external motivation we give them eventually needs to transform into an internal drive. And it is important that you not be the one keeping your teen from taking control of their life. Paul wrote to the Thessalonians, "The one who is unwilling to work shall not eat." Provision can quickly become enabling. So be there for your teen, but don't let that keep them from accepting responsibility for their life and becoming motivated to take care of themselves.

*Fools find no pleasure in understanding but
delight in airing their own opinions.*

PROVERBS 18:2

Mom and Dad, your kids are dying for you to listen to their heart. Your teens live in a world where very few people listen. And they're trying anything they can to get someone to truly hear them. My encouragement to you is this: quit talking and start listening. Tonight at the dinner table, don't speak unless you're asking a question. And don't respond to your teen's answers. You don't have to react, Mom. And Dad, you don't have to fix anything that you think is broken. Even a fool appears wise when they keep their mouth shut. All you need to do is listen!

And we urge you, brothers and sisters,
warn those who are idle and disruptive,
encourage the disheartened, help the
weak, be patient with everyone.

1 THESSALONIANS 5:14

The middle school years are a tough time to endure. Our boys become little tough guys, and our girls enter into their drama-queen years. They're no longer "little kids," but they don't have the maturity or sense to be a "big kid."

These years are not for the faint of heart. It's going to take a lot of work to keep your soon-to-be teen focused and out of trouble during this highly influential time. It's going to take even more work for you to shift your parenting style to accommodate the new needs and respond to the new influences that your middle schooler will experience.

It's not a time to let go but rather a time to focus on preparing your child for the world they are entering. Pour your life into your middle schooler and commit to being an active participant who will help them get through these difficult years.

JUNE 14

Raise a banner on a bare hilltop, shout to them;
beckon to them to enter the gates of the nobles.

ISAIAH 13:2

What banner flies above your home? Is it a banner of condemnation? A banner of constant correction? A flag of conflict? Are there emblems of authority stuck on all your walls? Is there a signpost outside your home that says, "Leave your problems outside?" Are there warnings spoken and inferred that encourage perfectionism? Are pennants of judgment flying when conflict approaches?

Might I suggest another banner? How about the banner of love? One proclaiming that—regardless of the struggles, difficulties, mistakes, and screwups you've all experienced—everyone in your family is loved.

It's the right flag to wave. That banner of love is flown during times of peace and conflict. It's a banner of acceptance, inclusiveness, connectiveness, and belonging that tells a child they are welcome and always loved despite any differences they may have with you.

The name of the LORD is a fortified tower;
the righteous run to it and are safe.

PROVERBS 18:10

You can raise your teens to live in a zoo or train them to survive in the jungle. You're not getting rid of the Internet anytime soon. Nor are you going to do away with cell phones. And more importantly, you won't always be able to manage the way your teen tries to connect and establish relationships with others.

What you can do is take advantage of the opportunity you have to influence and train your teen. This means you've got to be very intentional about helping them use these technologies to connect with others responsibly and to do so in such a way that protects them from potential dangers and encourages discernment.

And the peace of God, which transcends
all understanding, will guard your hearts
and your minds in Christ Jesus.

PHILIPPIANS 4:7

I fear that the contrary and oftentimes confusing culture our children are living in is causing normal teenage angst to accelerate into an overwhelming and crippling sense of anxiousness. Couple that with a lack of genuine relationships and you have a perfect storm of insecurity and fear.

You can help by engaging with your teen and making sure you are preparing them for the world they're going to live in. Your presence in their life and affirmation of their greatest qualities can encourage them through most situations. Your involvement in their life speaks volumes, and your timely counsel can change the destiny of your teen's future. Remember the Scripture, "Be anxious about nothing," and give your teen hope to live that out in their life.

*But God will never forget the needy; the
hope of the afflicted will never perish.*

PSALM 9:18

Grief, hurt, feelings of loss, and anxiety are all part of a teen's life. But depression is a common and serious medical illness that negatively affects how your teen feels, how they think, and how they act. So don't ignore the signs of depression in your teen. It's serious. It's not something that will just go away on its own, and it can progressively get worse as the years pass.

Thankfully, depression is treatable. But it isn't cured by a few encouraging words, a fun walk around the block, or an adventurous vacation. It is cured by regular counseling, wise input, medication, and a safe setting for your teen to work through their feelings of despair and unhappiness. Don't ignore depression!

The fear of the LORD is the beginning of wisdom,
and knowledge of the Holy One is understanding.

PROVERBS 9:10

When yelling is present, listening isn't happening. There is an old Turkish proverb that says, "If speaking is silver, then listening is gold." That's so true, just like the passage in James that encourages us to "be quick to listen, slow to speak and slow to become angry" (James 1:19). That's easy to say but hard to live by when what we view as important isn't being taken the way we'd like.

If this is the case, you must change your style and realize that yelling will get you nowhere and will only push your teen further away from you and anything that you believe. What you are doing is setting an example of communication that will destroy your teen's future relationships with their spouse and your grandchildren. Yelling is a symptom of a lack of communication. So listen better, get some new tools into your parenting tool box, and learn to give a gentle answer.

But the eyes of the LORD are on those who fear
him, on those whose hope is in his unfailing love.

PSALM 33:18

Your kids used to think that you were perfect! That's when they gave you T-shirts and coffee mugs that said "World's Greatest Mom" or "World's Greatest Dad." And then they became teens, and your greatness began to be measured not by how perfect you are but by how you share your imperfections and how you've worked through struggles.

You'll never be perfect this side of heaven. And your teen knows it! So change how they perceive you. Start sharing your struggles and challenges, your hurts and blunders, and the difficulties you encounter with people. It will usher in a sense of hope that they, too, can make it through the hardships that are coming their way. Your teen will now love you more for your imperfections than your perfections.

Whoever walks in integrity walks securely.

PROVERBS 10:9

Most parents overestimate the value of their words and underestimate the effectiveness of their actions. They think that if they just talk more, then their teens would listen. Instead, they should be embracing the understanding that teens pick up more in what they see than what they hear.

Many teens can't hear a word their parents are saying because their parents' actions are speaking too loudly. There must be consistency in the words you speak and the actions they see. It's called integrity, and it's this integrity that sets an expectation that says, "Don't just talk like me. *Be* like me." Don't just "talk the talk"; be intentional in how you "walk the walk." Your "withness" is your most effective witness.

A hot-tempered person must pay the penalty;
rescue them, and you will have to do it again.

PROVERBS 19:19

Sometimes a teen needs to experience life rather than just hear about what it's supposed to be like. These experiences give validity and value to the wisdom you are speaking into their life and move them to embrace the biblical principles you have placed in their heart.

Scripture reminds us that if you rescue an angry man once, you'll just have to rescue him again. With that in mind, let your teen experience consequences, pain, hurt, disappointment, and loss so they can see for themselves how important it is to make good choices and wise decisions. If you always interfere and circumvent the learning process, you are just postponing that lesson to a later time when consequences will be greater and affect more people. Training up your child includes helping them navigate the challenging and painful experiences they will encounter.

In their hearts humans plan their course,
but the LORD establishes their steps.

PROVERBS 16:9

*B*elieve it or not, your teen wants structure. Just as man plans his steps and God directs his path, your teen wants a trail to follow where they can make decisions along the way. It is parents who clear the path, put up fences to keep them from going over the edge, provide lighting in the darker areas of the trail, and motivate the teen along the course.

Reminding a teen of the purpose for walking the path becomes an opportunity for encouraging (not nagging) them to attain their goals. And giving insight on those actions that would take them off the path is also important, if given as reassurance and not ridicule.

Your role is to help your teens get to where they want to go. Now, where do they want to end up?

May your unfailing love be with us, LORD,
even as we put our hope in you.

PSALM 33:22

*I*f you have an adopted child, you might face some challenges that have origins you cannot quite pinpoint, and
you may wrestle a bit with how to approach these issues.
If your child is starting to question things that seemed
"buttoned down" in the past, it does not mean that something is wrong. Quite honestly, it's normal.

It is because your teen is beginning to see their adoption from a different perspective, and they are trying to find
answers to feelings they have never had before. You can
help your teen process these new thoughts and feelings and
lead them to a better understanding of the beauty of adoption and your choice to bring them into your family.

Blessed are those who find wisdom,
those who gain understanding.

PROVERBS 3:13

Your teens are longing to know how to take what you have taught them in life and apply it to their world. The best form of communication is not your wordy lectures; it is the blameless example that you live before them. They will be drawn to you by the life they see, then listen to the words they hear.

You've got to shift your style from a teaching model to a training model, where you empower them with godly wisdom and not just more of the earthly chatter they are bombarded with daily. Quit throwing out more information, and start sharing wisdom through the life you live and the conversations you have. Listening to their heart provides a far greater opportunity to influence your teen than those eloquent lectures that accomplish nothing. You possess the wisdom they need!

Let perseverance finish its work so that you may
be mature and complete, not lacking anything.

JAMES 1:4

I know that you do not want to be an overprotective parent
or grandparent. I've never heard anyone say that's their
goal. And I've never heard a parent say that they would not
like for their teen to be prepared for the world. But I have
seen countless teens fall flat on their face upon graduating
from high school because parents weren't intentional about
preparing for the post-teen years.

Your teens want to know how to manage their world
and how to take all you have taught them and apply it to the
opportunities before them. So stop protecting all the time
and start preparing them for the challenges they'll face. Let
them fail and learn, make decisions and reap the results,
and take charge of their life and be "mature and complete,
not lacking anything."

*Children are a heritage from the LORD, offspring
a reward from him. Like arrows in the hands
of a warrior are children born in one's youth.
Blessed is the man whose quiver is full of them.*

PSALM 127:3–5

No one said this parenting thing was going to be easy, did they? If they did, they had no idea what they were talking about. The challenges really have more to do with you than with your child. You'll learn that you must shift your style of parenting, learn about their new world of influence, and pursue your teen in a relational way that isn't marked by anger and disappointment.

By making your child your most important investment, you'll have done all you can to ensure that you'll continue to have an influence in your child's life. You'll give them a taste of the character of God and the assurance that your love for them is something they can depend on for years to come.

*A brother wronged is more unyielding
than a fortified city; disputes are like
the barred gates of a citadel.*

PROVERBS 18:19

*F*orgiveness is required so that relationships can flourish and not become stuck in the foolishness of adolescence. Scripture tells us, "A brother wronged is more unyielding than a fortified city." It's normal to want to shut down and walk away from those who have hurt you. But God's love empowers us to muscle through the hurt and take the higher road of forgiveness. That gives the recipient a taste of something that you and I have experienced: forgiveness from God. We are to parent our teens with the same kind of grace that God demonstrates toward us. It's an example of a relationship that is full of forgiveness.

My son, do not despise LORD's discipline,
and do not resent his rebuke, because
the LORD disciplines those he loves, as
a father the son he delights in.

PROVERBS 3:11-12

*R*ules are a part of life! They are essential for teaching your child the concepts of authority, obedience, and discernment. Your child may not like them, but rules are critical for helping your him or her develop into maturity.

Having a willingness to play by the rules is such an important life lesson to learn during adolescence. Your child needs your rules to help them know which path they should choose and what road to not take. Help your teen by giving them some rules to live by—not a million of them, but just enough so they know your boundaries and expectations.

As for me, I will always have hope;
I will praise you more and more.

PSALM 71:14

Your kids will find relief from anxiety, depression, and despair. My prayer for you is that they'll do so in positive and healthy ways. But with the ever-growing presence of marijuana and alcohol, chances are your child will become exposed to these things during their teens.

So have the conversations early (starting around the fifth grade). It's not only about getting them to "just say no"; it's about connecting with them in such a way that you'll be able to spot a sense of hopelessness before it starts to overwhelm your child and before you feel as if you're losing the son or daughter you once knew. Your relationship with your teen is of utmost importance. Perhaps it's the very thing that will keep them from choosing a path of destruction.

Know also that wisdom is like honey for you:
If you find it, there is a future hope for you,
and your hope will not be cut off.

PROVERBS 24:14

Grandparents, whether they show it or not, your teen grandchildren need your involvement in their life. They don't need to hear about your medical issues or how everything was better "back in the old days." They need to hear the wisdom you have gathered throughout your life so they can know how to apply some of it to theirs. Your teen grandchildren need your love, your wisdom, your encouragement, your listening ears, and your compassionate heart. Give them perspective, create a home of rest, and listen with attention. God has a message to give your grandchildren through you. Go find out what that is and give your grandchildren something they can receive from no other person.

Give thanks to the LORD, for he is
good; his love endures forever.

PSALM 107:1

Over time, unconditional love can melt the coldest of hearts. Teens have an amazing way of thinking that their performance and appearance will determine their value and the love they receive from others. While this may be true in the culture they live in, you and I know that is not the mentality we want our teens to embrace. Our teens need those constant reminders that bring them back to the reality that our love for them is unconditional. So tonight, let your teen know that there is nothing they can do that will change your unconditional love for them.

I instruct you in the way of wisdom
and lead you along straight paths.

PROVERBS 4:11

*A*t some point, your teen will get in an argument with
you. It is their way of learning how to express their
feelings, put words to their sometimes-crazy thinking, and
form dialogue that shows their passion and desires. It can
be healthy if they argue with a sense of respect. And this is
what I've found: parents show their teens how to argue by
their example. That example should be one that is founded
on the words of James: "Be quick to listen, slow to speak
and slow to become angry" (James 1:19). What a great
Scripture to encourage patience and compassion.

Take advantage of the opportunities that arise when
your teen wants to argue. Help them learn to do it well so
they understand how to communicate clearly and do so in
a way that doesn't damage relationships.

When you pass through the waters,
I will be with you; and when you pass through
the rivers, they will not sweep over you. When
you walk through the fire, you will not be
burned; the flames will not set you ablaze.

ISAIAH 43:2

Your teen is designed to connect with people. I also know that teens go through periods of curiosity that might appear foolish and rebellious. When these two realities meet, it's easy to think that other kids are responsible for negatively influencing your teens. That can be the case, but it's not always so.

But just as teens influence one another, you have an opportunity to be a positive influence in the lives of your child's friends. Perhaps God has placed these "bad kids" in your backyard to be around you. Spend more time being an influencer than one who thinks you must protect your child from other teens who do not have it all together. You might just find that you have a whole new mission field.

You, my brothers and sisters, were called to be free. But do not use your freedom to indulge the flesh; rather, serve one another humbly in love. For the entire law is fulfilled in keeping this one command: "Love your neighbor as yourself."

GALATIANS 5:13–14

History has taught us that independence usually happens as a result of a battle. The battle is yours to fight, knowing that the result of your efforts will help a teen become motivated to take responsibility for their life. This means you must learn to back away, give room for your teen to begin acting independently, and help them mature and develop so you don't have to baby them the rest of their life. Many times it's harder for a parent to let go than it is for a teen to take responsibility. You'll find that, as they mature, your relationship will deepen. While they may make some mistakes along the way, you'll enjoy the adult they are becoming because you have pushed them to do so.

My son, if your heart is wise, then
my heart will be glad indeed.

PROVERBS 23:15

There's nothing that will make a mom or dad more proud than when they watch their teen demonstrate wisdom rather than foolishness. And that wisdom they display by their actions comes from a heart that has truly been changed.

Scripture reminds us that a foolish son is a grief and anguish to his father and bitterness to her who gave birth to him, so it's natural to think that if a son is wise then a father's heart would be glad.

Here's the catch: foolishness comes easy; wisdom does not.

Your role as a mother or father is to shift the emphasis of your training by sharing more wisdom in your discussions, your actions, your shared perspectives. Take the wisdom you've learned from being in different situations and share it with that teen, who naturally acts and believes foolishly.

*But to each one of us grace has been
given as Christ apportioned it.*

EPHESIANS 4:7

As I've said before, grace is moving toward your teen and offering them your relationship when they've done something to damage that connection. But because of your relationship with Christ, you have been empowered to love beyond your feelings and hurt and to love unconditionally. That's what you can offer your teen in the midst of their poor choices and decisions.

It's an offer of relationship, not a reprieve from consequences. It is your relationship with your teen that will ultimately change your their heart and behavior. Move toward them when you want to move away, and show them a love they'll not see anywhere else. It's loving your teen just as God loves you.

*Get wisdom, get understanding; do not
forget my words or turn away from them.*

PROVERBS 4:5

Your teen will be affected by the world's influence, and that is why it's so important to understand the need to be a counterbalance. Their concept of what is permissible, what modesty looks like, and what relationships are about really comes from you. Their acceptance and application of those principles you have taught them hinge on how you approach the challenges brought on by this ever-changing world.

Thinking that your teen won't be influenced by the culture they live in is naive. And to believe that they will always make the best decisions is lofty indeed. When they do fall, don't ruin a lifetime of influence with a response that pushes your teen further into their sin. Love on them the same way that God loves on you when you don't make the best of decisions. Your response can make all the difference in the world.

*Rooted and built up in him, strengthened
in the faith as you were taught, and
overflowing with thankfulness.*

COLOSSIANS 2:7

Grandparents, you have a special role in the life of your teen grandchildren. You are not to be a parent on steroids; you are a grandparent, one who can offer what you've gathered throughout your life and share that unique wisdom in a way that makes your grandchildren long to be in your presence.

Your challenge will be relevancy. Your goal is to remain engaged. And when these two things connect, your grandkids will observe and reflect on your life in a way that pours wisdom into theirs—something you possess that they are earnestly searching for. So make your home a place of rest, let your words be ones of encouragement, and create a relationship with your grandkids that is unlike any other, giving them a taste of the character of God and an example of a life well-lived.

They are new every morning;
great is your faithfulness.
LAMENTATIONS 3:23

You play a much more important role in the life of your teen than you will ever know. It is because of you that they will feel value, purpose, and direction. You will be the one to direct their path as they plan their steps. You set into motion a life that is purposeful and significant. It's important that you have a healthy relationship with them.

The first thing to do is be healthy yourself. Know the path that you want to walk so you can understand what is needed to help your teen walk along that path with you. The second important thing is to pursue a relationship with them the way God pursues one with you.

You will be secure, because there is hope;
you will look about you and take your rest in safety.

JOB 11:18

Your child's success or failure is usually determined by whether they're allowed the opportunity to take a risk and assume responsibility for their actions. This may mean you need to give up control or let them make some decisions. Or it may mean letting them learn the hard way and develop a greater sense of maturity by getting knocked around a little. It's your response to the failures they experience as they assume more responsibility for their life that will let them know it's better to try and fail than to never try anything at all.

Take advantage of the opportunity to teach your teen how they can bounce back from a failure. That failure is not the end of the world; it's how they learn the need to listen to advice and gather wisdom. Teens will learn from their mistakes, but only if you give them permission to do so.

*Carry each other's burdens, and in this
way you will fulfill the law of Christ.*

GALATIANS 6:2

*P*robably one of the greatest challenges for moms and dads is how to manage the impact of the Internet and social media within their family. You are pioneer parents, learning how to wade through the sea of technology available to your teens. You can spend your time complaining about the evils of the Internet, or you can spend time helping your teen navigate those waters.

Mom and Dad, you play an important role as technology becomes more and more central to your teen's culture. And that role, primarily, should be to give them a taste of what a real relationship looks and feels like. You aren't going to be able to protect your kids from all negative aspects of technology and the Internet, but you can counter the effects they're having on your family by setting an example and relating without the use of a phone or a computer.

"For where your treasure is,
there your heart will be also."

MATTHEW 6:21

Your teen knows that you love them. And I know that they love you. But sometimes that message gets lost in the busyness of life, and it's not until there's a train wreck that we all wake up to the need to be involved in one another's lives. If your teen is struggling, then you have to change your strategy and begin engaging differently if what you're currently doing isn't working.

If you are not involved in their life, that void will only be filled by other people and things that will never satisfy the need they have for you. So change it up, try something different, set a new course, and let your teen know that you want to be a part of their life in a new way.

*The fear of the LORD is the beginning of
wisdom; all who follow his precepts have good
understanding. To him belongs eternal praise.*

PSALM 111:10

*I*f you don't let your teens take responsibility for their lives, they'll find areas to show you that they have the ability to make their own decisions. If you're controlling all the "good" areas of their life, they'll stoop to "bad" areas to prove they're in control. Their bad behavior is more about taking charge of their life than it is about violating your values.

Your teens want to make choices and begin exercising more control. If you don't give them the opportunity to develop in this way, they'll take it anyway, and usually in ways that are hardly pleasing to parents who uphold biblical standards and principles. Let the rope out easy as they age, and you'll find that they are capable of making good decisions if you help them and give them opportunity.

*The LORD is good, a refuge in times of
trouble. He cares for those who trust in him.*

NAHUM 1:7

Sometimes kids who need the most love will ask for it in the most unloving ways. And those unloving actions are usually the cause of conflict in your home. Go beyond focusing on the undesirable behavior and be sure to get to the root of the issue. When you begin to understand what is really going on, you will find that you might be able to resolve conflict by speaking to the heart of the issue, and your teen will deescalate when they see that you are pursuing their heart, not just correcting their behavior. Resolving conflict is never easy, but it's better when your teen realizes that you're not fighting with them but for them.

*The father of a righteous child has great
joy; a man who fathers a wise son rejoices
in him. May your father and mother rejoice;
may she who gave you birth be joyful!*

PROVERBS 23:24–25

D o your teens know what your expectations are, and do they know the consequences for violating those expectations? Most teens I know want to know what is expected of them. I think your teens want the same.

Teens want structure. It acts as a set of guardrails that helps them achieve their goals and desires and protects them from making poor, wasteful, and even destructive decisions.

And remember, rules without relationship is a recipe for rebellion. But relationship without rules causes chaos. Whenever you try to implement rules or change the current ones, make sure that your relationships are healthy and that everyone understands the purpose of the requirements you are putting before your teens.

"Bring them to me so I may bless them."

GENESIS 48:9

*I*f you're lucky, your parents are involved in the lives of your children. Proverbs says your "children's children are a crown to the aged." And grandparents, God isn't keeping you alive just so you can play a little more shuffleboard or have a few more rounds of golf. He wants you to be involved in the lives of your grandchildren so you can share all the wisdom you've gained and speak it to a generation that is in such need of guidance and direction. You are needed greatly, so pour your life into your grandchildren and give them a blessing they'll receive nowhere else.

*The law of the LORD is perfect, refreshing
the soul. The statutes of the LORD are
trustworthy, making wise the simple.*

PSALM 19:7

One of the greatest tasks you will be given is helping your child move from dependence on you to independence and putting into practice all you have taught them. I know you love your kids and want to help them in any way you can. While well intended, your provision may be the very thing that is keeping your teen from a successful launch and may be enabling their immaturity. Whatever stage you're at with your adolescent, be intentional about helping them to accept responsibility for their life and to learn to make the choices that will bring about the maturity they long to achieve and that you long to see in them.

*"Peace I leave with you; my peace I give you.
I do not give to you as the world gives. Do not let
your hearts be troubled and do not be afraid."*

JOHN 14:27

*L*oving your child when they're doing everything right is pretty easy. It's when they begin making mistakes and bad decisions that it becomes a little harder. God calls you to love them the same, regardless of their poor choices.

Sometimes I think the disappointing choices teens make are just screams for someone to notice and engage with them at a heart level. So when you see behavior that you thought you would never see in your child, commit yourself to making sure you don't withhold your love from your teen when they need it most.

You will be enriched in every way so that you can
be generous on every occasion, and through us
your generosity will result in thanksgiving to God.

2 CORINTHIANS 9:11

Sometimes getting your teen to talk is like pulling teeth from a mouth that's been wired shut.

Before you can get your teen to talk, they must feel that their environment is safe and free from ridicule. Your son or daughter must know that there is an opportunity to openly express feelings and that there's a benefit for them in even having a conversation. You can't use the same communication style with your teen that was effective in their earlier years. It just won't work.

The inviting atmosphere you create will produce the conversations you desire. Just make sure you are not the one who is preventing communication from happening. Reflect, invite, and sit back and listen.

My goal is that they may be encouraged in heart
and united in love, so that they may have the full
riches of complete understanding, in order that
they may know the mystery of God, namely, Christ.

COLOSSIANS 2:2

*T*eens are growing up in a world where they communicate more with their fingers than with their mouth. So to expect them to converse the way we did, well, it just doesn't happen that way anymore.

A little conversation to us is *a lot* of conversation to them. If too much of a good thing does harm, then perhaps your discussions can be in smaller doses. Choose your words carefully, and make sure your conversation partner understands the motivation behind your efforts.

Whatever you do, don't disengage from your teen. They really do want to have talks with you; they just don't know how to get them started and keep them rolling.

*Hope deferred makes the heart sick, but
a longing fulfilled is a tree of life.*

PROVERBS 13:12

*P*ain has an amazing way of teaching some great lessons to your teens. It's a part of training and a part of life. Hard experiences push teens to search for wise answers. It's important to allow your child to experience pain, hardship, difficulty, and consequences while they're still living under your roof so that you are present to speak truth and wisdom into their life, preparing them for days ahead when they will encounter similar and even greater challenges. These temporary painful challenges just may be designed by God to produce endurance and character and bring hope to your teen.

Join together in following my example, brothers
and sisters, and just as you have us as a model,
keep your eyes on those who live as we do.

PHILIPPIANS 3:17

No parent really desires to have a "failed launch," where a child just can't make it in the real world and begins to flounder rather than flourish. If your teen never blasted off, you now hold the key to making sure that you are not the cause of their lack of growth. You are now instrumental in helping them move out of the zoo and into the jungle.

Your actions must help this process, not hurt it. You can begin by withdrawing financial support, but never withdraw your relational support. As you let them know that it's time for them to take control of their life, also let them know that you'll be with them and will help along the way. When do you start? Right now.

Finally, all of you, be like-minded, be sympathetic,
love one another, be compassionate and humble.

1 PETER 3:8

*I*t's more than likely that teens today change because of relationship rather than because some strong arm of the law pounds them into shape. Cultural changes have greatly affected teens' learning processes and have forced every parent to use different tools to encourage their child to learn from mistakes and pursue the wisdom necessary for a successful life.

The authoritarian approach works well in a child's younger years, but it sometimes backfires during adolescence. Begin today to make that switch from an arm that pushes to one that embraces. That will help you become successful in training your teen to face the difficulties and hardships presented by their culture.

I wait for the LORD, my whole being
waits, and in his word I put my hope.

PSALM 130:5

When you feel like hope has left the building and things can't get any worse, you're really at a good spot to make the changes your family needs, because there's nowhere to go but up. The light of hope can be found in the darkest of places, so don't give up; instead, commit to a plan that reinforces the truth that your family can't live like this anymore.

Sometimes the best feeling in the world is watching things fall into place after watching them fall apart for so long. Now's the time to make those changes and turn your family's ship around and into the right direction.

To answer before listening—that is folly and shame.

PROVERBS 18:13

Hearing and listening are two vastly different actions. Listening requires that you seek the heart of what's being said and pay more attention to trying to understand than thinking about how you're going to respond. It means being intentional about hearing the heart of your teen, which goes deeper than just hearing the words they speak.

If your teen makes comments like "That's not what I mean" or "You don't understand" or "That isn't what I said," then help them know that you want to listen, and give them another chance to help you understand. Say, "I don't think I understand what you're trying to tell me; help me." You'll be surprised how they want someone to just listen.

Do not repay evil with evil or insult with
insult. On the contrary, repay evil with
blessing, because to this you were called
so that you may inherit a blessing.

1 PETER 3:9

You have an opportunity to convey your never-ending love for your teen when you catch them lying to you. Deep down, they really need more than the consequence you feel they need to suffer because of their dishonesty.

You must understand that teens lie for a reason. And the reason could be that you haven't created an atmosphere where they feel comfortable sharing the truth. Remember, you set the atmosphere that they live in. So take the opportunity to get to the bottom of why they lie and don't want to tell the truth. When you get to that point, a teen will begin to see the value of telling the truth and understand that relationships grow when deceit is absent.

*Therefore, as God's chosen people, holy and
dearly loved, clothe yourselves with compassion,
kindness, humility, gentleness and patience.*

COLOSSIANS 3:12

Your adopted teen is more than likely fighting feelings of rejection from their birth mother, and they may not even know why they feel the way they do. It's because they're starting to think differently: they're moving from concrete to abstract thinking, from embracing the facts of the past to facing the unanswered questions of the future. This is a time when they are wrestling with why they were abandoned and given up. It doesn't mean they don't love you; it means they don't understand why someone would not want them. You can be a great help to them during this time by showing that even though someone did indeed give them to you, they were valued enough to become a part of your family. Allow both feelings to exist, and allow them to wrestle through this thing called adoption. Your love will eventually win over their doubts.

Fools give full vent to their rage,
but the wise bring calm in the end.
PROVERBS 29:11

When parents and teens are angry with each other, it's usually because both aren't getting what they want. A teen wants something to happen their way, and a parent wants there to be respect, calmness, and conformity. Each side hates it when it doesn't go their way.

So handle it a bit differently when you see your teen getting angry. Have a discussion. Ask some questions. Try to understand their viewpoint. And give yourself some time to back up and think through what your teen is wanting. This short period of time allows you to be sure of your thinking and gives some time for your teen to cool off so they can hear your plan for how you both can get what you're looking for.

Your approach will model a way of dealing with conflict that ushers in change, moves you into a deeper relationship, and brings about the righteousness that God desires.

Accept one another, then, just as Christ
accepted you, in order to bring praise to God.

ROMANS 15:7

Summer should be a fun time. It's a season to live life without a focus on academics and the social pressures that school brings. It's a time to shift gears, to reevaluate what your home life is going to look like for the next couple of months, and to put into place some expectations for where you want your teen to be by the end of summer: fully rested, with a few more dollars in her bank account, more independence, more privileges, and hopefully a deeper relationship with everyone in the family.

Accomplishing these goals doesn't just happen. I would encourage you to do something different this summer. Be realistic in your expectations, and be available to spend time deepening your relationship with your teen.

Turn from evil and do good;
seek peace and pursue it.

PSALM 34:14

If you have a teen who is deep into drugs, they are literally screaming for help by their actions even though you may never hear a word from them about it. A teen who has taken a plunge into the drug world—and I'm talking about drugs far more dangerous than marijuana—is doing so because they have lost hope and don't know how to get out of the hole they've fallen into.

This is where you must quit fighting *with* your teen and start fighting *for* your teen. This life-and-death situation must be battled now, and you must seek help from others who have the expertise and knowledge to help your teen crawl out of that dark hole. You must stop at nothing to get your child the help they need from either a drug treatment program or a counseling and support group that will instill a sense of hope back into their life. The time to act is now!

Let us therefore make every effort to do what leads to peace and to mutual edification.

ROMANS 14:19

Moms and dads (and all you grandparents as well!), the boundaries you have laid out aren't just house rules—they are your personal rules. Boundaries ensure that everyone knows what is yours and what is not yours, what you will allow and what you won't, how you will and will not be treated, what your schedule will look like, and how you'll spend your money. Boundaries define who you are and who you are not.

Boundaries are for you! They are established fences that let all know where you begin and where you end. They are just as important as the rules you set for your home, if not more so. They define you and protect you from being walked on by others. It's not selfish to create boundaries. It's necessary! If you don't set boundaries, how will your teens ever have any?

Consider the blameless, observe the upright;
a future awaits those who seek peace.

PSALM 37:37

Your teens need grandparents in their lives—not to just buy them things and take pictures but to be involved in their lives and to share wisdom and insights. You have the ability to influence your grandchildren if you remain engaged and relevant. I'm not saying to just dump everything on them whenever you want. What I am encouraging you to do is to first listen and then share what you have gathered through your own observations, reflections, and experience.

Let your discussions be guided by what they want to talk about. Create a place of rest for their weary souls. Quit focusing on rules and emphasize the relationship. Your legacy will not be determined by what you leave in their bank account but by what you have deposited in their hearts. You have a place in your grandkids' lives, and it's a very important one.

Peacemakers who sow in peace reap
a harvest of righteousness.
JAMES 3:18

If You've been wanting more time with your teen and now you have it, take advantage of the opportunity before you, no matter how challenging it may be. You will be the one setting the atmosphere of your home by displaying your character and genuineness through your actions, which speak a million times louder than your words ever could. You have the opportunity to model for your teen how to be a peacemaker who pursues truth and love in the midst of argument and division. So take advantage of what's been placed before you and let your teens see that love you've been telling them about for years.

*Rejoice always, pray continually, give
thanks in all circumstances; for this is
God's will for you in Christ Jesus.*

1 THESSALONIANS 5:16–18

The grandkids who live far away can't wait to see me, and they come running whenever this graying man walks toward them. I can even hear them smile when I call them on the phone. The challenge is to keep their admiration growing as they age and expand their social circles, which I hope will continue to include me.

The time they will need me the most is not during their preteen years but in their adolescence, when their culture gets a little crazy and they need a large dose of wisdom to get through that time unscathed. On my part it will take intention, purpose, regular contact, and actions that display a love they can get from no one else. Listening, caring, encouraging, and spending time are the greatest ways to let them know I love them dearly. What better traits could I be remembered for?

*I will listen to what God the LORD says; he
promises peace to his people, his faithful servants.*

PSALM 85:8

Your teens are looking for a safe harbor amid the storm where they can refuel and be understood. They are looking for a place of rest, a place where they can recharge, where they can be genuine and authentic, where they can take a break from the craziness of a culture that seems bent on destroying the very principles and values we embrace.

I hope they can find that kind of sanctuary in your home. The rules and expectations you set in their preteen years have worked well and got you to where you are now. But if you don't relax on those rules and expectations, your teens will never able to relax. And if they can't unwind at home, they'll find other ways to get away from it all. Everyone needs a break; maybe it's time you give your teens one.

*If it is possible, as far as it depends on
you, live at peace with everyone.*

ROMANS 12:18

*B*elieve it or not, your teen needs and wants you in their
life. But what they don't know is how to create that
environment where a deeper connection can flourish. This
is where they are relying on you to make that happen. You
set the tone of your home. You determine the atmosphere.
You make it a comfortable place where they want to be or
a place where they can't wait to get away from. Your home
can be a haven of relationship that affirms and encourages
or a setting that pushes them far away. Creating an inviting
space doesn't just happen. It is built with a goal in mind and
an intent in your heart. Tonight, do this one simple thing:
ask your teens how you can make your home a place they
want to be with you!

*Make every effort to keep the unity of
the Spirit through the bond of peace.*
EPHESIANS 4:3

*I*f I spent all my time correcting the teens who live with us, I would never be able to develop a relationship with them. As your teen gets older, you'll find that the only way they'll listen to you is if you have a connection with them. This is what will allow you to gain the podium of influence you long to have in their life.

With that connection, you'll find that they'll be coming to you to ask for your help, your wisdom, and your insight. Without it, you'll be just another dripping faucet that irritates your teen and causes them to look for a connection in anyone but you.

The LORD is my strength and my shield;
my heart trusts in him, and he helps me.
My heart leaps for joy, and with
my song I praise him.

PSALM 28:7

Uncertainty induces fear, which can lead to panic pretty quickly. It can cause a teen to misuse their imagination and worry about life and doubt those things you have taught them throughout their childhood. Once anxiety about the future begins to run rampant, a teen quickly loses hope.

So here's my encouragement for you today: you are to be a voice of certainty in uncertain times. You can either fuel the worry and panic, or you can be a calming voice that turns a bad situation into a wonderful opportunity to see how God is going to show up in the days ahead.

If you build deeper relationships in times of uncertainty, you can be sure of the certainty of those relationships in the days ahead.

A friend loves at all times, and a brother
is born for a time of adversity.
PROVERBS 17:17

Your teen needs an ally, not another enemy. Believe it or not, they want to resolve the conflicts in your home and in their life. And to do that, they need you!

Your willingness to enter conflict with your teen sends a clear message that you are willing to risk having some uncomfortable discussions for their benefit, and it communicates that you love them even when you're in the middle of a conflict with them.

Your willingness to talk about disagreements lets them know that conflict is a part of life, and they'll learn that the quicker they work through issues for the sake of a relationship with someone, the happier they will be.

Let us love one another, for love comes from God. Everyone
who loves has been born of God and knows God. Whoever
does not love does not know God, because God is love. This
is how God showed his love among us: He sent his one
and only Son into the world that we might live through
him. This is love: not that we loved God, but that he loved
us and sent his Son as an atoning sacrifice for our sins.

1 JOHN 4:7–10

When you boil it down, the essence of what we should be about is love. As I look at all my Christian tradition, Scripture memory, worship, and learning about the character of God, I find that it all funnels into the way we love: the way we love Him and the way we love others. My prayer for you is that you are not just a resounding gong or a clanging cymbal in your home. I hope you are love personified because of the One who lives in you and gives you the ability to offer that love unconditionally.

Whether it's your spouse, your parents, your children, your neighbors, or anyone else in your life, I pray that you can be that beacon of light in their lives that lets them know you will always love them without wavering. May your relationship with others flow from the new person Christ has made you to be.

But the fruit of the Spirit is love, joy,
peace, forbearance, kindness, goodness,
faithfulness, gentleness and self-control.
Against such things there is no law.

GALATIANS 5:22–23

Helping your teen deal with anger is one of the greatest life skills you can help them develop. You can be the greatest example of temper management or the worst model of explosive anger; either will be mimicked by your teen. So be careful how you respond when things don't go your way—you're being watched.

Their anger is a warning light on the dashboard that flashes when they're not getting what they desire in life or from relationships. It is your opportunity as a parent to determine what is fueling the anger and to get to the heart of the issue by asking questions that transcend their behavior, which is only the visible expression of the invisible issues in their life. It's okay for your teen to be angry as long as it doesn't control them, lead them to be disappointed or jaded about life, or cause them to act inappropriately in relationships.

They must turn from evil and do good;
they must seek peace and pursue it.

1 PETER 3:11

It's hard to believe that another school year is starting. You know, kids get five chances throughout their teen years to have some "do-overs." With that in mind, make sure you stay engaged during this time. Ask questions, participate in discussions, and spend a lot of time listening. If your teen is to mature a little more each year, it means that you've got to allow that to happen: expanding their horizons, allowing greater exposure, encouraging more academic responsibility, and transferring more control of their life to them. This is all part of the "training process"—a process that can strengthen your relationship and allow you to be involved in every part of your child's life.

LORD, you establish peace for us; all that we
have accomplished you have done for us.

ISAIAH 26:12

Your teens want to be at home, and they want to have a place where they can relax and feel part of a family, because that's how God designed us. So what should you do? The first step to creating a place where your teen wants to be is to ask why they don't want to be there now. Once equipped with that knowledge, you can move on to make the necessary changes.

This doesn't mean that there aren't chores to do, responsibilities to fulfill, and requirements for living at your home. But it does mean that you create an atmosphere of relationships that is attractive for their friends, one where connection is more prominent than correction. It's a challenge (and it always will be) to keep the temperature of your home steady in an ever-changing culture.

*Therefore, if anyone is in Christ, the new creation
has come: The old has gone, the new is here!*

2 CORINTHIANS 5:17

Your teens want to go deeper; they just don't know how. You have the opportunity to show them how to engage at a deeper level. The first decision you have to make is whether you really want to go deeper in conversation and relationship, because this will push you to go deeper in your own life and force you to examine areas that have maybe never been addressed. But your teen will love you for it. As they get older, they want to have deeper relationships, and the best chance of that happening is with you.

So strip away the old and bring in the new. Let them know that you want to move from the shallow end of the conversation pool. It's a longing and a hope fulfilled when you take your teen to a new place of relationship.

He will wipe every tear from their eyes.

REVELATION 21:4

I believe that loss is one of the greatest motivators for teens. Perhaps what they once had is gone, what they thought they would have never materialized, or something they hoped for was never fulfilled. Loss is the chasm in the heart caused by deprivation, failure to achieve something, or possibly a defeat. It is the hollowness and loneliness that remains when something is taken away.

Your teen's behavior may be motivated by a desire to fill a void in life or to replace something that has been lost. The character traits of a lifetime, both good and bad, are often developed in the all-but-forgotten events of childhood. When you find out what's driving your teen's behavior, you'll be able to get to the heart of the issue.

*My prayer is not that you take them out of the
world but that you protect them from the evil one.*

JOHN 17:15

Your teen will have the opportunity to use some type of gateway drug in their life, so it's extremely important that you realize your teen's choices may lead them and the entire family down a deadly path that no one wanted to walk.

There are two things to watch for. One is the opportunity available to your teen. Drugs are accessible, permissible, and, many times, promoted by those who don't care about your child. So keep your eyes peeled. Second, if you suspect that your teen is using, get the help they need quickly. Don't just try to change their behavior; help them understand that the choices they make today *will* affect their life tomorrow. Encourage them to use their head, make good choices, and walk away from those desires that appear attractive but are ultimately deadly.

A fool spurns a parent's discipline, but
whoever heeds correction shows prudence.

PROVERBS 15:5

There is a risk in letting your teen make more decisions in their life. And that risk might include times when they don't use their best judgment. But they are learning how to make good decisions, and you must allow them to do so, even though they will make mistakes.

They will blow it and disappoint you, but you must have courage and give them another opportunity to exercise their decision-making muscles. It means that you have to give them another chance to blow it again for the sake of learning lessons. Let them make choices and be responsible for their decisions, and have faith that the process will develop a sense of maturity in them.

*For lack of guidance a nation falls, but
victory is won through many advisers.*

PROVERBS 11:14

Teens get lost. It's easy for them to do so in a world where choices are plenty and wise counsel is scarce. You have to be that voice of wisdom and reason that speaks out to your teen when they're doing well but also engages with them when they are not. It's called unconditional love: staying with them whether they're on the right path or they stray onto a road that leads them someplace undesirable.

Staying with your teen during this time in their life will be your witness to them. So go after the lost one, and let your child know that you will never take your eyes off them. Your steady, loving guidance will set them up for a victorious life.

For each one should carry their own load.

GALATIANS 6:5

Start telling your children early on that they need to take responsibility for their life. Too often we want to be in charge of our teens. But for every instance that we're in control, we're missing the opportunity for our kids to learn this essential life skill for themselves. We have authority as parents in the preteen years, but during adolescence we hope to see them make the transition to exercising their own agency and taking on greater responsibility.

Many times, because of our desire to retain that feeling of control, we lose a lifetime of influence. Teens want the opportunity to take responsibility. Let them have it, and communicate to them that "from everyone who has been given much, much will be demanded." Your teens will love the freedom and will begin to learn what it is to become an adult.

*You, therefore, have no excuse, you who pass
judgment on someone else, for at whatever point
you judge another, you are condemning yourself,
because you who pass judgment do the same things.*

ROMANS 2:1

You're not perfect—you never have been and never will be this side of heaven. So quit trying to appear to be something you're not. When you do, you release your teen from the pressure of needing to have it all together and never making a mistake. Perfection in this life doesn't exist, and your attempts to be perfect don't send the message that being who you were created to be is a far greater accomplishment than appearing perfect.

The bottom line is that your teens need an atmosphere where the demand for perfection is low and the encouragement to be honest is high. Authenticity creates a connection and a deeper relationship that helps them become who they were designed to be.

For the Spirit God gave us does not make us
timid, but gives us power, love and self-discipline.
2 TIMOTHY 1:7

Parenting a blended family can be a tough spot to be in, and the challenges that you'll face are unique to the new family you've put together. Let me encourage you with a couple of thoughts that might help.

First, if you believe that all that comes to you has first passed through the hands of God, then the challenges you face are going to be a wonderful (though not always fun) opportunity to learn how to accept what is before you and how to lean on Him for your strength and guidance.

Second, the challenges of step-parenting will soon pass. As you and your spouse grow closer, time will pass, and the challenges presented by blending your family will soon be in the rearview mirror. So hold on to each other, trust that God is present, and take advantage of the opportunities before you.

Those who know your name trust in you, for you,
LORD, have never forsaken those who seek you.

PSALM 9:10

If your relationship with your teen has become distant, it is more than likely that the slow drift began long before you realized it. It's going to take a little effort and the passing of a few seasons to get that "drifter" to come home.

Let me encourage you to reflect on ways you can make your home more of a haven of blessing for your teen so that they will be drawn to reengage and deepen their relationship with you. It won't happen overnight, but in time your efforts will be seen as an olive branch offered in the hope of healing a relationship that has a lifetime of value. Keep moving toward them, just as your heavenly Father constantly moves toward you.

*"Though the mountains be shaken and the hills be
removed, yet my unfailing love for you will not
be shaken nor my covenant of peace be removed,"
says the LORD, who has compassion on you.*

ISAIAH 54:10

Your commitment to developing a stronger relationship with your teen, regardless of the circumstances, is an admirable effort to demonstrate to your child the steadfast love that God has shown to you. Pursue the relationship, admitting where you've been wrong and changing anything on your part that is getting in the way of diving further into relationship with your child.

Deal with the heart of the issues your teen has, not just the behavior that you see. The issues resolved today won't come back in the future, and this will allow your teen to grow through their adolescence with a healthy perspective of life and the relationship you have built with them.

"I have told you these things, so that in me you may have peace. In this world you will have trouble. But take heart! I have overcome the world."

JOHN 16:33

Your teen likely believes that this world is the worst it could ever be, because that's what they hear, and it's the only life they've been exposed to. Their feeling of being inadequately prepared to live and function in their world quickly turns to worry (misuse of one's imagination), then fear, and then anxiety. If anxiety is allowed to fester, it can turn into panic, a feeling of terror they are certain cannot be overcome. They find a retreat from those pressures and look for peace amid the conflict by disconnecting and isolating.

It's a tough spot to be in when your teen feels the world is crushing down on them, but it's also your opportunity to share perspectives of the world to help them understand that much of the fear and turmoil they feel will soon be over and that you are there to walk with them until it passes. It's not a time to share your opinions; it's an opportunity to listen and be a steady source of comfort for your anxious teen.

*"You are the light of the world. A town built on a hill
cannot be hidden. Neither do people light a lamp
and put it under a bowl. Instead they put it on its
stand, and it gives light to everyone in the house."*

MATTHEW 5:14–15

*T*eens are growing up in a tough world. Criticism, ridicule, and negative comments about those in authority are pervasive. Disrespect is around every corner, and it's almost unavoidable. The fact that some of it rubs off on your teen should not really be that much of a surprise.

Your role is to give them a reason to respect others and to be an example of someone to respect. The way you engage with those who disagree with you is an opportunity to shine in the midst of the contemptuousness swirling around us all. Your response to the world must be as a light in the darkness and a gentle voice in the chaos. Let your teen see the assurance of someone who refuses to be affected by those who live out of a critical and disrespectful mindset.

*Wash away all my iniquity and cleanse me from
my sin. For I know my transgressions, and my sin
is always before me. Against you, you only, have I
sinned and done what is evil in your sight; so you are
right in your verdict and justified when you judge.*

PSALM 51:2–4

If your teen is pushing you away, they're doing so for a reason. And one of the greatest challenges of parenting is to understand why a son or daughter who has been given so much is walking away from the ones who love them the most.

Want to know the truth? It's probably something you are doing that doesn't sit well with them, or it's something you are not doing that they would love to have as a part of your relationship. Your job is to figure out which one it is, put them first, and make the change in the only person you're able to change—yourself! It's asking the Lord to search you, give you a test and know your anxious thoughts, and help you see if there is any hurtful way in you. This is about connecting and reconnecting, and you have to take the first step toward your teen.

"The thief comes only to steal and kill
and destroy; I have come that they may
have life, and have it to the full."

JOHN 10:10

Today ushers in a new opportunity for you to be that beacon of hope and instill a sense of confidence in your family and your relationships. Focus on living with anticipation and courage. Don't let any election, pandemic, or any other thing tempting to weigh you down rob you of the joy of an abundant life. Your hope should not rest on anything external; it must come from within because of the new person you are in Christ. Let your light shine so brightly that it radiates to your family and encourages a sense of hope as they face a world filled with fear and despair.

No one has ever seen God;
but if we love one another, God lives in us
and his love is made complete in us.

1 JOHN 4:12

*I*f you're struggling with your teen, chances are you're also struggling a bit with your marriage. The turmoil with your teen might just be taking attention away from other members of your family, including your spouse.

I would encourage you to avoid getting angry because things aren't working the way you want them to. Let the disappointment move you to find new paths of engagement with your spouse. The way your teen is disrupting your schedule can be frustrating, but you must find other ways to connect with your spouse. Battles with your adolescent don't have to produce collateral damage to a once thriving and happy marriage.

Affirm one another. Encourage time together. Get away when needed. Be open and honest about feelings. That means you too, Dad! This temporary challenge will soon be behind you, and your marriage will survive.

May the favor of the Lord our God rest on us;
establish the work of our hands for us—
yes, establish the work of our hands.

PSALM 90:17

Summer is finally over, and a new school year is beginning. What happens over the next few weeks will determine the atmosphere for the upcoming year. So remain engaged. Keep talking, spending time together, and making sure that your teen is staying on track. The new academic year also gives you a chance to start anew, forgetting the past and pressing on toward a greater year.

Your teens are under more pressure than you ever were at school. And the relationship they have with you will ensure a successful and productive upcoming year. You have only a few of these years left, so take advantage of the time and find new ways to engage with your teen. They really need your support.

*You make known to me the path of life; you
will fill me with joy in your presence, with
eternal pleasures at your right hand.*

PSALM 16:11

*D*epression and anxiety are not like a headache that
will just go away. Nor are they problems that a pill
alone will totally fix. These problems demand serious
attention for the teen who is suffering from them. First off,
your teen doesn't want to feel this way, whether they are
severely depressed or overly anxious. They don't like it, but
they don't know how to get out of the dark hole they find
themselves in.

Second, they need a community of help—from
you, from their church, from family members, and from
someone who can help steer their thoughts and guide their
discussions to get to a healthier place.

This isn't a time to fix your teen. It's a time to be
there with them as they struggle through this season of
adolescence.

*I have been crucified with Christ and I no
longer live, but Christ lives in me. The life I now
live in the body, I live by faith in the Son of
God, who loved me and gave himself for me.*

GALATIANS 2:20

Anger is a normal response to any disappointment, hurt, or missed expectation. And if there's ever a time in life when someone will experience any one of these, it's during adolescence. Your teenager will display anger, and it will be important for you to help them avoid becoming angry in the first place by not letting them set their expectations too high, by stopping their entitlement hopes, and by helping them understand that one doesn't always get what they want.

Selfishness plays a big part in anger. Helping your teen become selfless is key to avoiding unrealistic expectations and standards that can pave the way for destructive outbursts. Your example of how you handle anger and the depth of your relationship with your teen are key ingredients in helping them control their anger and not hurt people.

Therefore, I urge you, brothers and sisters,
in view of God's mercy, to offer your bodies
as a living sacrifice, holy and pleasing to
God—this is your true and proper worship.

ROMANS 12:1

Grace is hard. It's hard to extend the hand of relationship when it seems as if your teen is doing everything they can to destroy what you have built through the years. And it's hard to move toward someone when they are pushing all your buttons.

If your teen is losing their way, Scripture would remind you to go after that child who is walking away and to pursue your son or daughter just as God pursued you when you were lost.

When your teen has hurt you by violating your values, keep the relationship. When your daughter has said hurtful things to you, keep the relationship. When your son embarrasses you by some foolish action, keep the relationship. When your teen knows you will never leave them, it speaks louder than any words you could ever say.

The LORD himself goes before you and will be
with you; he will never leave you nor forsake
you. Do not be afraid; do not be discouraged.

DEUTERONOMY 31:8

One is a lonely number. And there's nothing worse than a teen who feels like they have no friends, doesn't have anyone to turn to, and can't see the future as being any different from what they're experiencing right now. Kids are created to be in relationship, and they are desperate when they cannot enjoy what they've been created for. In that desperation, they may make poor choices and display some inappropriate behavior.

The root of their behavior may be a sense of loneliness that they're trying to overcome. Lonely and secluded kids may feel abandoned and deserted. You can be the one who reaches through the loneliness and assures them that you will never leave them, just as your heavenly Father has never left you.

*Therefore we do not lose heart. Though outwardly
we are wasting away, yet inwardly we are
being renewed day by day. For our light and
momentary troubles are achieving for us an
eternal glory that far outweighs them all.*

2 CORINTHIANS 4:16–17

You don't walk on water, and neither does your teen. And the demand that he is expected to do so has a potential of damaging your relationship. Yes, you should encourage striving for excellence. And you should want good things for your teen and have expectations they can reach. But you should also give them room to fail, make mistakes, and not have it all together.

Your teen wants to know, more than anything else, that they are just as loved when they have it all together as when everything is falling apart.

The atmosphere you create determines the type of relationship you have with your teen. While you encourage and challenge your teen to do great things, allow genuineness and authenticity to be the norm in how you relate to them.

*I have no greater joy than to hear that
my children are walking in the truth.*

3 JOHN 1:4

*H*onesty is a character trait that is cultivated in a home that values it. You are the ones who create that setting where truth (good or bad) can be shared and where discussions can happen without the beginning of World War III. Deceitfulness destroys, so make sure you address the dishonesty you see, but do so after you've created an environment where everything can be put on the table and your teen knows that your love for them will not be diminished by one thing that they might say. Truth sometimes hurts, but regardless of who feels the pain, it is truth that moves your family into deeper relationships with one another and affirms your love for one another.

Therefore, since we are surrounded by such a great cloud of witnesses, let us throw off everything that hinders and the sin that so easily entangles. And let us run with perseverance the race marked out for us.

HEBREWS 12:1

The challenge of every parent is to determine what is motivating your teen, asking why they do what they do and then getting to the core issue that your child is trying to solve. The parent who comes alongside their teen to help them attain a goal will be way more effective than the one who is concerned only with stopping certain behaviors. As always, you do this by conveying the message that nothing they do can change your love for them in the slightest. It's a message that your teen not only needs to know but needs to experience from you as well!

Be alert and of sober mind. Your enemy
the devil prowls around like a roaring
lion looking for someone to devour.

1 PETER 5:8

I know forty-five teens who have taken their own life. No
one saw any of these tragedies coming. The prevalence
and sometimes promotion of this act in our modern culture
gives teens permission to believe that taking their life is a
viable option to escape the struggles they have in their life.
Here are some key takeaways I have for you: (1) Your teen
is capable of taking their life. (2) You have got to be aware
of what your teen is thinking and feeling. (3) If your teen
is struggling, or if you even think they're struggling with
suicide, get help. Please take me seriously when I tell you to
seek help if you ever suspect that your child is suicidal. Your
actions can save the life of your teen.

Jesus said, "If you hold to my teaching,
you are really my disciples. Then you will know
the truth, and the truth will set you free."

JOHN 8:31–32

In a world where many relationships seem plastic and misrepresented, your teen is looking for authenticity in those around them. You are the first line of influence to give them a taste of what it is to be real, valid, dependable, and faithful; you have the power to counter the fake imagery and stories put before your teen. The ability to share your struggles and reveal your hurts and pains shows your strength in what you believe and in whom you believe. God didn't call us to live fake lives. He's called us to be real and true.

This is the time to get real, the time to be who you were made to be. When you demonstrate what it means to be genuine, your teens can learn to be comfortable in their own skin and enjoy how they have been created.

The LORD God took the man and put him in the
Garden of Eden to work it and take care of it.

GENESIS 2:15

I've learned that teens need to have a job as soon as they
are able. The valuable lessons they pick up in the work-
force will mold a responsible and mature young man or
woman, one prepared to enter a world apart from Mom
and Dad's home.

A job eliminates a sense of entitlement. It shows your
teen that how they invest their time has value, and it helps
them understand the world they are about to enter. And if
your teen is good at their job, it can set the course for their
future, and they might even learn a lesson about why people
are fired from their job, just as I did at Tennessee Jed's.

The first thing God did with Adam was give him a job.
He told him to take care of the garden. Perhaps by encouraging your teen to have a job, you will initiate their journey
into maturity and developing into a responsible adult.

Humble yourselves, therefore, under God's mighty
hand, that he may lift you up in due time.
Cast all your anxiety on him
because he cares for you.

1 PETER 5:6–7

We all make mistakes. Sometimes that's really hard to acknowledge. It's hard to let your teens know that you've made a mistake when you're trying to be an example and to be blameless among them. Hey, you're human.

And when you admit your humanity to your teens, you let them see that it's okay to share your imperfections. Admitting mistakes and wrongdoings is a path to wisdom and an opportunity for you to create an atmosphere of acceptance for those who make mistakes. If you shift your parenting style to give them more control of their life and encourage them to make more decisions, you must also let them know that your relationship isn't governed by their mistakes. What better way to do that than to admit your own?

He will not always accuse, nor will he harbor his
anger forever; he does not treat us as our sins
deserve or repay us according to our iniquities.
For as high as the heavens are above the earth,
so great is his love for those who fear him.

PSALM 103:9–11

Do you get frustrated when you don't see change happening within your family? Are you waiting for your teen to make their move, or are you trying to figure out what you might have to accomplish in your home that would allow that change to happen?

Your teen wants change—constantly. Very few are comfortable with doing the same thing over and over. But they just don't know how to implement the change they want to see. It's your role as a parent to develop an environment that welcomes change and grows along with your child to meet their new needs. Transformation will begin to take place when change is adopted as a family value.

Now finish the work, so that your eager willingness
to do it may be matched by your completion of
it, according to your means. For if the willingness
is there, the gift is acceptable according to what
one has, not according to what one does not have.

2 CORINTHIANS 8:11–12

Someone once told me that I need to write a book about expectations because problems in relationships are usually caused by the expectations we have of others to meet our desires. We must strive to put the other person's interest first, figure out what they want and need, and work to help them meet their expectations of themselves, not try to get them to live up to our expectations of them.

You naturally want good things for your teen. Help them to embrace those good things, and spend time finding out what their desires are. You'll help your teen get further in life by helping them meet their expectations of themselves rather than getting them to live up to yours.

If we confess our sins, he is faithful and
just and will forgive us our sins and
purify us from all unrighteousness.

1 JOHN 1:9

I've found that teens really do want to share about their life if they believe their family is able to handle what they have to share. I would encourage you to work hard to create an open and warm environment so that when your teen puts their toe in the pool of vulnerability, they will want to jump in with both feet. I've found this to be true: teens actually want to be found out so they can be held accountable, stop behaviors they know they shouldn't be doing, and start pursuing things that are healthy and productive.

It's their choice whether to open up, but it's your responsibility to create an environment where sharing thoughts, admitting wrongdoings, and being honest is welcomed and something to be admired. And it begins with you creating the setting for that to happen.

But you, Lord, are a compassionate and gracious
God, slow to anger, abounding in love and
faithfulness. Turn to me and have mercy on me;
show your strength in behalf of your servant.

PSALM 86:15–16

It always amazes me that the teens who stay with us at Heartlight come to live with a group of other "bad teens," the ones that parents don't want their kids to hang out with. But in the process of growth, they learn about deep relationships in a way they've never experienced before and now long to have for the rest of their lives. So is it the bad kids who are responsible for undesirable behavior?

I don't believe that "bad teens" are the issue; the issue is whether they can be loved in such a way that they experience something they want for the rest of their lives. That first taste might just be the way that you love them, with the same patience and compassion that God showed you during your "bad days."

Direct my footsteps according to your
word; let no sin rule over me.

PSALM 119:133

There is a motivation behind your teen's behavior. They do things for a reason. All their behavior is the visible expression of the invisible issues swirling around within them. It's your job to figure out what that motivation is and engage on a level that goes beyond dealing with the behavior and gets to the heart of the issue so you can put a stop to inappropriate actions. It's not just tearing off the top of the weed but digging down to get the roots so that the weed will never sprout and grow again.

Your task is to get to the root of the matter. Don't ignore bad behavior; it must be dealt with. But the long-term results of doing the hard work of digging deeper will prevent inappropriate behavior from raising its ugly head in the future.

*If we claim to have fellowship with him
and yet walk in the darkness,
we lie and do not live out the truth.*

1 JOHN 1:6

The role you play during your child's teens may be the most important and influential one of their lives. Most parents never realize the significance of the example they're setting, so they never embrace the need to spend time not only "talking the talk" but also "walking the walk."

If you're one of those parents who believes that the power of your parenting lies chiefly in the words you share, then you'll never have as much influence as those who not only share the gospel but share their lives also as they engage with their teens. Your teen needs a living example of the biblical truths you have taught. They need to see the Word of God fleshed out in you, and they desire to see a life that is full of truth and grace, one that doesn't walk away when they make mistakes.

But he said to me, "My grace is sufficient for
you, for my power is made perfect in weakness."
Therefore I will boast all the more gladly about my
weaknesses, so that Christ's power may rest on me.
2 CORINTHIANS 12:9

We all experience losses, and we all respond in so many different ways. I can guarantee that your teen won't respond to losses the same way you do. Most parents spend way too much time dealing with the behavior produced by losses in a teen's life and don't spend nearly enough time dealing with the actual loss an adolescent has experienced.

Focus on the behavior, and you'll postpone resolution of your teen's issues to a later time. Focus on the loss, and you'll change their heart, change their behavior, and change the trajectory of their life. If you deal with the empty spaces your teen is trying to fill with their inappropriate behavior, you'll deepen your relationship with your brokenhearted teen. Be to your teen who God has been to you, and love them in ways that He has loved you.

For where you have envy and selfish ambition,
there you find disorder and every evil practice.

JAMES 3:16

The world of comparison that your teen lives in can steal the joy out of their life. They may be angry that their world just isn't turning out the way they had hoped, and their display of anger is an emotional response to not getting what they want. Your efforts to control how they respond to a situation, while ignoring the real message behind the anger, will sometimes only cause that anger to grow.

When your teen is angry, they're really showing you what they want and what they don't like. It's a perfect opportunity to dive deeper into their thinking and help them process it so they can get to a better place. Help them learn that they can be angry and respectful at the same time.

Brothers and sisters, if someone is caught
in a sin, you who live by the Spirit
should restore that person gently.

GALATIANS 6:1

Teens self-medicate for a reason. So while it's important to set boundaries, develop rules about substance abuse, and determine consequences for using, it's equally imperative to determine the reason they're turning to these substances in the first place. Whether it is to fit in, mask issues in their life, manage a medical issue, deal with losses and hurts, connect with others, or to no longer feel the way they do, there's a motive behind their actions.

Get to the core issue and find the motivation for their behavior. They really do want help. And I guarantee they would like to discover other ways to get out of the hole they find themselves in. You can start by setting up boundaries, having those tough discussions, and letting your teen know of your never-ending love for them.

Not only so, but we also glory in our sufferings, because we know that suffering produces perseverance.

ROMANS 5:3

Sleepless nights, worry-filled weekends, random outbursts, and verbal shutdowns are never welcomed actions in this parenting thing, but it is a part of adolescence for many. Stay the course and hold fast to what you know is right. These times are producing something in you and are giving you an opportunity to enter into the parts of your teen's life that hurt the most. Take advantage of having a presence in the midst of the situation. Don't walk away or ignore what is before you. Walk toward those issues, believing that God is going to show up in a very special way.

*For the Son of Man came to
seek and to save the lost.*

LUKE 19:10

Chances are that your teen is more lost than rebellious. And if they're lost, I can assure you that's not a place they want to be. If they knew how to find their way on their own, they would. If you're a mess because your teen is going through a tough time, I promise you that your teen is more of a mess than you are, and this is when they need you the most.

They may not say it or even act like it, but there is no one more capable of helping a teen find their way than parents who stick with their teen, for better or worse. Your investment in their life during this time will make all the difference in the future of your family. Demonstrate grace to your wayward teen and remember that you, too, were once lost but now are found.

But thanks be to God, who always leads
us as captives in Christ's triumphal
procession and uses us to spread the aroma
of the knowledge of him everywhere.

2 CORINTHIANS 2:14

I'm convinced that the quality of a great parent-teen relationship can be measured by the amount of time parents listen and the amount of time teens and parents can laugh together.

When parents are intentional about listening in order to understand rather than to find fault or to correct, it displays a genuine concern for their child. Honestly, you just might be the only person who is really listening to the heart of your child. Moms, you have a sixth sense that can understand the depth of your teen's heart. And dads, you have the ability to sift through the meaningless to get to what is purposeful. I encourage you to use those gifts to listen to the heart of your teen. Don't just hear them when they speak; listen to their heartbeat, just as God does with you.

Surely God is my help; the Lord
is the one who sustains me.

PSALM 54:4

Conflict has an amazing way of smoothing off the rough edges of life. Most times, this can only be seen after the conflict is resolved. Conflict is a precursor to change. It gives us the opportunity to challenge a current way of thinking with a resolve that will put any family, any parent, and any teen on a better course for the days ahead.

So, if you have conflict going on in your family, don't ignore it. Speak to that elephant in the room, even if you don't know how to resolve what is before you. Sometimes, just identifying that the elephant exists, allows others to know that you're not afraid to "work through" the hardships or struggles that you see before you.

Identifying the conflict is the first step to moving to resolve, to making those changes in your family that you have been wanting for years. Now is the time to face what has been unfaceable in the past.

Trust in the LORD with all your heart
and lean not on your own understanding;
in all your ways submit to him, and
he will make your paths straight.

PROVERBS 3:5–6

When you ask questions about your teens, you're seeking answers that just might help you in your parenting quest. If you ever find yourself thinking, "I don't know what to do," or if you feel that you don't have the answers, that is a wonderful place to begin a search for what will be effective in your teen's life.

Don't stay in the dark. There are plenty of resources waiting for you that will answer those questions keeping you up at night. Whether it's about disrespect, cell phones, your past mistakes, or your teen dating, don't lean on your own understanding, but search for answers that will continue to keep the connection with your teen.

To fear the LORD is to hate evil; I hate pride and
arrogance, evil behavior and perverse speech.

PROVERBS 8:13

There's nothing more difficult than moving toward a teen and offering them your relationship when they are hating you, hating God, and being prideful and arrogant. Those behaviors would make anyone want to walk in the opposite direction.

But that may be when your teen needs you the most.

That's the time when you need to be gracious and move toward them. It's not an easy thing to offer when you've been offended. You must remember that teens change because of relationship, and if they can't have that with you, it'll be a tremendous challenge for them to ever have a loving relationship in their lives.

A loving relationship doesn't love only when all is going well. It's that special kind of bond that sticks around even when all is not so well. It's loving even when everything the other person is doing is unlovely and nothing they're doing makes you want to walk toward them. Taking the first step and reaching out may be daunting and uncomfortable, but your heavenly Father will equip you with everything you need to restore this relationship.

*Sin is not ended by multiplying words, but
the prudent hold their tongues.*

PROVERBS 10:19

Your teen is constantly bombarded with followers and likes and friends and shares. Never has a generation had so many contacts but so few relationships. This is where you can come in and engage with your teen on a deeper level to help them understand what a real relationship looks like.

They need your depth more than your constant correction, and they need your wisdom a lot more than they need more information. They need your listening ear rather than you rattling off the next great lesson to teach them. They need you, and that will happen when you find time in both of your busy schedules to sit down, eat some ice cream, and listen to the heart of your teen.

You will be amazed at their desire to be with someone who is committed to having some one-on-one time.

But if you suffer for doing good and you
endure it, this is commendable before God.

1 PETER 2:20

Right choices don't always bring about good results. I've known well-meaning parents who appeared to have done everything right in raising their teens, and the end result has been nothing but a mess at best. These parents stood up for what was true, based their decisions on godly principles, and participated in every aspect of their teen's life, yet their child still took off on a different path.

There's no parenting equation that says if you just do a, b, and c, then it will equal something wonderful. This is where the suffering comes in—suffering when you've done everything correctly, and the right side of the equation isn't really fair.

Keep doing right and holding on to what you know is true. Don't measure your efforts in parenting by the outcome of your teen. There are times when you'll do everything right, and in the short run, you'll see nothing but suffering. If that's the position you're in now, continue persevering and trust that God will bless your faithful sowing.

*If this is so, then the Lord knows how to rescue
the godly from trials and to hold the unrighteous
for punishment on the day of judgment.*

2 PETER 2:9

I've always held to the belief that anything and everything
that comes to us has first passed through God's hands.
Part of that is believing that whatever comes is meant to
transform us more and more into the person God desires
us to be. I believe that, but I don't always understand it.

It is at those times that I decide just to leave it up to
God: to His timing, His purpose, and His lesson that He
wants me to learn. It's then up to Him to determine when
He's going to show me the answer to the questions that
cross my mind.

It's all in His timing when He wants to rescue me. My
role is to glean as much as I can from the trial before me
until the time of my rescue, always searching for the lesson
that He wants me to learn.

And a voice from heaven said,
"This is my Son, whom I love; with
him I am well pleased."

MATTHEW 3:17

All parents have to ask whether their teen truly knows that they are loved—not the kind of "I love you" that ends a conversation or is said in passing but the kind of love that a teen knows at their core. That genuine communication can happen in the middle of a heated exchange or in the silence of a moment. Whenever and however it is communicated, your child needs to know there is nothing that can keep that river of love from flowing into their life.

The second part of your messaging may be a little harder, and that's communicating that you are "well pleased" with your son or daughter, even when you may not be. It's at those times that a wise parent speaks the truth in love about what they're not pleased about.

You can love a teen and not be happy with their behavior. You must separate the two. "I love you. Period" is the message you must give them. God may not always be pleased with the choices we make, but He never withdraws His love for us.

*Turning your ear to wisdom and applying
your heart to understanding.*

PROVERBS 2:2

*I*f you want your teens to talk to you, you've got to bridle your speech and develop your listening skills. They have listened to you during their preteen years. Now it is time for you to listen and to take that first step of getting them to come to you for the wisdom you can offer. Instead of giving answers, ask more questions. Replace your lectures with discussion. Offer wisdom instead of blurting out information. Commit to using your ears a lot more than your mouth. Listen with the intent to understand, not to reply. Use silence as a tool to get them to pursue you. You might just be surprised at how much they want to talk with you if you would just quit talking at them.

*"But love your enemies, do good to them, and lend to
them without expecting to get anything back. Then
your reward will be great, and you will be children of
the Most High, because he is kind to the ungrateful and
wicked. Be merciful, just as your Father is merciful."*

LUKE 6:35-36

Grace is getting a blessing we do not deserve, and mercy is not receiving a punishment or consequence that is rightfully ours. The hardest time to apply either of these concepts to your family life is when your teen's friends are taking them down a path that you'd prefer they not be on. When trying to figure out what to do in this case, grace is usually not what comes to mind, and the idea of mercy doesn't seem just.

So what are you supposed to do? Have you ever thought that God might have placed those "other kids" in your life so that you can have an influence on them? That maybe your teen is the conduit to a group of friends that needs your influence?

You can try to engage rather than disengage. You can make an approach rather than walk away. Maybe try to connect rather than disconnect. If your teen's friends are the cards you've been dealt, then play the hand and see what happens. You might just be surprised.

We love because he first loved us.

1 JOHN 4:19

There isn't a parent I know who really thought their child was going to commit suicide. This act of hopelessness many times comes out of nowhere. Know that every teen is capable of taking their life, and your child is no exception.

Your teen lives in different worlds—one within your family and the other in the social world of their peers. Teens can be so disrespectful and hateful to one another, so it's best to keep a finger on the pulse of your child's social life. Remain involved, and constantly look for ways to show interest in not only their life with you but also the life they carry on with the peers around them.

God's kindness is intended to lead you to repentance.

ROMANS 2:4

*T*eens don't change because of a bold display of authority in the midst of an argument. Nor do they positively respond to comments, opinions, or remarks that they feel are judgmental. Nor do they feel compelled to do better when they sense a hint of a demand for perfection.

Here's when they listen: when you demonstrate a genuine, caring attitude that is reflected in your tone and when you listen fully to what's on their heart.

Teens respond to a relationship. It's the small rudder that turns any "big ship" conversation around. Relationship is the spark that creates a warm and inviting fire to sit by where the more difficult issues of life can be discussed.

It all begins with kindness. Ask your teens how they think you're doing with that character quality. You'll have a very different type of discussion around the dinner table tonight.

*"If you, then, though you are evil, know how
to give good gifts to your children, how
much more will your Father in heaven
give good gifts to those who ask him!"*

MATTHEW 7:11

It's easy to select gifts to give on birthdays and holidays. I always wonder what gifts to give to others throughout the rest of the year. For me, it's usually a relational gift: the gift of listening, the gift of keeping my mouth shut, the gift of spending more time connecting, the gift of rest. They're all things that can be given on any day of the year.

What gifts have you given your teens lately? If you're giving relational gifts, doing anything possible to dive deeper into a connection with your teen, then commit to offering a new one every day. There are many ways you can show grace to your teen by giving of your time, attention, and energy. When you share these gifts, give them freely!

Don't you remember that when I was with you . . .
2 THESSALONIANS 2:5

Your most powerful witness is your "withness." If you are the most spiritual person in the whole world but don't spend any time with anyone, then what good is your light if it's hidden under a bushel? Scripture would remind you to let your light shine before all so that they may see your good deeds.

Your presence in the life of your teens is the greatest gift you could ever give to your family. That means adjusting your calendar to accommodate the priorities of others and being present with your teens when you are spending time with them.

Teens feel supremely valued when you desire to spend time with them and make them the focus of your attention. Your "withness" lets them know that they have priority in your life. I can guarantee this: one day, in the not-too-distant future, you're going to miss the days when you had the opportunity to participate in their lives. Your "withness" is the most important part of your parenting.

When I am afraid, I put my trust in you.
In God, whose word I praise—in God I trust and
am not afraid. What can mere mortals do to me?

PSALM 56:3–4

One of your greatest challenges as parents is trusting God and His plan for your family when things within the home aren't going the way you expected. It's easy to trust when all is going well; it's a little harder when your teen isn't following the path you had hoped, and their choices don't quite line up with your values.

It's easy to be confident when giving advice to another struggling family, saying, "He who began a good work in you will carry it on to completion" (Philippians 1:6). It's harder when it's happening in your own family.

God hasn't left you. Nor is He ignoring you. In a mysterious and maybe even odd way, He's giving you the opportunity to learn a new approach to loving and embracing your family. The conflict you're experiencing may open the door to a much-needed change.

Take advantage of the time to reflect, to figure out your role in the conflict, to determine the needs of your teen and the heartbeat of their life. This is the time to trust that God knows what He's doing and to not be afraid of the deepening relationships that will come out of this current crisis.

But the LORD is with me like a mighty warrior;
so my persecutors will stumble and not prevail.
They will fail and be thoroughly disgraced;
their dishonor will never be forgotten.

JEREMIAH 20:11

It's so easy to want vengeance and payback on those who've hurt you. At the same time, carrying around that desire for retaliation can eat you up and cause more damage to you than the initial incident. The roots of bitterness and hate are hard to pull, and the fruit of such trees drop seeds in other areas of your life.

Here's where you have to let it go. I'm not talking about forgetting and acting as if nothing happened. It's letting go because you know that the Lord Himself is a mighty warrior who is more than capable of handling any situation in your life. Scripture charges us to repay no one evil for evil, and it reminds us over and over of God's capabilities. Let Him do what He does, and you focus on what you need to do.

Though your riches increase, do
not set your heart on them.

PSALM 62:10

Scripture tells us that where our treasure is, there our heart will be also. Treasure is what we value above all else, that which motivates our behavior. Some people seek money, some fame, some power, and some collect things and gather stuff that will remain behind when they move on.

The older you get, the more you'll realize that there's no greater treasure than family. As you age, you'll discover what is worth pursuing and what is not worth sacrificing family for. Perhaps gray hair and a few wrinkles are reminders about the passing of life and the need to pour one's focus into the greatest earthly treasure—family.

Would you put your family at the top of your priority list? Do you pour your heart into the relationships with your family members? Believe me, they are more important than money, fame, power, collections, or any other pursuit you could have.

Discipline your children, for in that there is
hope; do not be a willing party to their death.
PROVERBS 19:18

If we plan our steps and God directs our path, then we must do the same for our teens. Let them plan their steps along a path that we have set out for them. If we don't map it out for them, then they are left wandering through their adolescent years without a sense of direction.

It all comes down to learning about their goals and helping them get to their destination. With this plan, you are no longer keeping them from growing up but have now become an ally in their journey who will help them reach their target objective. Helping your teen achieve their desires and steering them away from pitfalls and distractions is one of the most important roles you can play in their life.

Do not hold against us the sins of past
generations; may your mercy come quickly
to meet us, for we are in desperate need.

PSALM 79:8

Generations have a way of carrying on damaging styles of communication, perpetuating unhealthy traditions, and covering up family secrets that ought to be dealt with. These habits sometimes have a way of keeping healthy relationships from developing, and they trap family members in a dark silence that operates under the guise of protecting the tribe.

These patterns don't protect. They prolong the pain and prevent healing from happening by never allowing restoration to happen.

Does your family have deep, dark secrets that could be resolved and redeemed by bringing them to light and allowing God's grace to reign over them? There's no better time than the present to deal with them. Perhaps today is a day of restoration, redemption, and renovation for your family.

For with much wisdom comes much sorrow;
the more knowledge, the more grief.

ECCLESIASTES 1:18

It's a simple concept: the more I know of a person, the more I am saddened by the tragedy, struggles, and sin in their life. As I get older more, I enjoy the good things around me, but I also can't ignore the sinfulness of myself and others.

At that point I must make a decision to either open my heart to the sadness of those around me or confine my feelings and worldview to that which makes me comfortable. It's a choice that will either move me to help those who are living a sorrowful story or help me build an emotional wall of protection. One is a life of selflessness, the other is a life of selfishness.

What choice will you make?

For the LORD is good and his love endures forever;
his faithfulness continues through all generations.

PSALM 100:5

Remember that all behavior is goal oriented. Everything your teen does is for a reason, and cutting and self-harm is no exception. If they are doing this to beat themselves up, then you might want to have a long discussion about your expectations of them and why they feel like they don't measure up. If their motivation is a cry for help, then spend time asking about their needs so you can get someone else like a counselor involved in their life.

Whatever the reason for self-harm, it is an action that cannot be ignored. The act is rooted in wrong thinking and is done as a way to find relief. These actions require the help of a counselor who can help find the root cause and help your teen develop new skills of coping with their world. The time to act is now.

*The way of fools seems right to them,
but the wise listen to advice.*

PROVERBS 12:15

No parent really wants their teen to go through suffering, but if pain is God's megaphone to a deaf world, it just might be what's needed to wake your child up to the world they live in and help them see the need to develop the skills required to survive in it.

The more responsibilities you give them, the more they can flex their decision-making muscles and learn how to carry the heavier loads they'll need to manage when they are no longer under your roof. Exposure to society in their earlier years allows them to hone the skills needed to flourish in the world.

If you trust what you have taught them and trust God's involvement in your teen's life, you will help your child become prepared for their future life.

*Later Jesus found him at the temple and said
to him, "See, you are well again. Stop sinning
or something worse may happen to you."*

JOHN 5:14

*I*t takes no effort to get worse, but getting better always seems to be a struggle. The things I want to do are what I have the hardest time doing, and the things I don't want to do, I find myself doing. Getting better consists of making good choices over a period of time that accumulate into healthy results. That is why it is so important that we teach our teens early on to start making wise decisions.

It's the choices a child makes that determines their success in life. The slightest bad choice can lead your teen down a path that only gets worse, but the slightest good decision can put your teen on the path of success.

Spend time helping them make wise decisions and letting them suffer the full consequences of the unwise ones so they'll develop the ability to choose and the strength to follow through.

*Blessed is the one who perseveres under trial
because, having stood the test, that person
will receive the crown of life that the Lord
has promised to those who love him.*

JAMES 1:12

Going through struggles with your family is tough. It's not easy on you, and it's not easy on the one causing the problem. There are times when all you've taught seems to have been forgotten, relationships formed have deteriorated, and you feel lost and alone on some forgotten highway leading to further darkness. Family struggle is the hardest.

But know this: God has promised that He will finish what He's started. He will bring to fruition the seeds that have been sown in your life and the life of your child. The trials you're experiencing are temporary. And the child who seems so distant just doesn't know how to come back into relationship with you.

Hang in there. You'll get through this. You'll learn some amazing and lifelong lessons. In time, you'll see God's hand in it all, even though you may not see it now. He who has promised is faithful. Don't give up.

You, my brothers and sisters, were called to be free.
But do not use your freedom to indulge the flesh;
rather, serve one another humbly in love.

GALATIANS 5:13

Where do you go when you feel like you've been beat up? To whom do you turn in your time of need? Who replenishes your soul when you feel depleted? Is there a person in your life?

Let me ask you another question. Are you that person in someone else's life? You can be the example of Christ to your teens when they feel beat up, in need, or depleted. Be a reflection of Christ to them. Offer that refuge and let them know of your care for their heart and soul. The example you place before them will be the example they carry on to the rest of their relationships.

"This is what the LORD Almighty said: 'Administer true justice; show mercy and compassion to one another. Do not oppress the widow or the fatherless, the foreigner or the poor. Do not plot evil against each other.'"

ZECHARIAH 7:9-10

*O*ftentimes we use our authority to force teens to listen to us. There are times when we think that rules and consequences will surely change a teen's direction. Or we resort to yelling with intensity to get across an opinion or voice a concern. Sometimes we nitpick a person to death just to prove our point that we're right.

Scripture encourages us to administer true justice, allowing consequences to have their full effect on a teen's choices. But that doesn't mean we have to be mad or angry at someone for violating rules. It means they pay the price of their choices and we then show mercy, which means we're not always looking to nail them for their wrongdoing. We continue to act with a great sense of compassion, which keeps the relationship intact while they agonize over the consequences of their choices. Allow justice to happen, but always let it be tempered by a sense and display of compassion.

For we live by faith, not by sight.

2 CORINTHIANS 5:7

What I see and what I know may be two totally different things when it comes to trying to figure out my teen.

What I see is a child who is entitled, won't stay off her phone, uses language I've never heard come out of her mouth, is seen posting an inappropriate picture of herself, is becoming quiet, and hardly engages with the rest of the family.

What I might need to know is that my daughter lives in a culture where possessions and appearance mean everything. I might need to know that all her time on the phone is to fulfill what she's been created for—relationship—because she knows of no other way to connect. She may be saying things and sending pictures that are out of line with how she's been taught because her normal voice or image isn't getting the attention she desires. And her quietness and withdrawn spirit might just be an expression of her frustration with a culture that doesn't line up with what she believes.

The behavior you see is the visible expression of the invisible issues going on in her life. Chances are that if you pursue those inner issues, you'll have a better chance of positively affecting her outward behavior.

Remember how the LORD your God led you all the
way in the wilderness these forty years, to humble
and test you in order to know what was in your heart,
whether or not you would keep his commands.

DEUTERONOMY 8:2

Many times when struggling with a teen, it may feel like the battle has lasted forty years! But let's look at it from a difference perspective. Sometimes the most rebellious teen in the family may be the healthiest of all the family members.

Could it be that God is using your teen's struggles to grab your attention and teach you some lessons? Might He be using your son to show you how to engage differently and become more effective as a parent? Might He be using your daughter to challenge some of those ideas that worked well during the preteen years but are really causing problems now?

God will put you through experiences so that you can find out what's in your heart and learn some ways to become closer to your teen. Take advantage of the opportunity to grow along with your teen and usher in a new kind of relationship.

"By their fruit you will recognize them. Do people pick grapes from thornbushes, or figs from thistles?"

MATTHEW 7:16

A change of heart should be demonstrated by a change in your teen's actions. Let them show you how they feel and what they believe by giving them the opportunity to make decisions, show their actions, and take responsibility for their life when they reach adolescence.

You've spent years teaching. Now is the time to help them put all that knowledge into use and apply it to their life. The planting in the preteen years will show itself in the fruit of the adolescent years.

Mistakes will be made, but poor decisions will teach some great lessons. Your child's taking responsibility for their life will create the maturity you desire to see. And your discussions with them will grow deeper and deeper as you help them develop their faith.

You've been planting for years. Now it's time to experience the fruit of your labors.

God loves a cheerful giver.

2 CORINTHIANS 9:7

Give your stuff away! You'll not take any of it with you once you depart this world. So spend a little of your hard-earned funds and create experiences that will give your kids the opportunity to see you live life before them. Make some memories together that they will never forget.

One day you will wish you had spent more money on giving gifts. And you'll one day regret not going more places with your kids. Set an example of what it means to give it away. It's only money. Teach them how to live it up, give it away, and enjoy the time you have together. Live with no regrets!

We demolish arguments and every pretension that sets itself up against the knowledge of God, and we take captive every thought to make it obedient to Christ.

2 CORINTHIANS 10:4–5

We see the pressures, the temptations, the opportunities, the challenges, and the ways that technology has taken over our teen's life, and we quickly become grateful that our youth was not consumed by these same trials and distractions.

But here's the reality: our kids have to grow up in a world that is far different from what we grew up in. Because we realize their plight in this wayward culture, we should also have a growing empathy for the challenges they face.

That understanding should change our approach and move us with compassion to realize that most teens aren't being rebellious—they're just lost. I don't know about you, but the minute I forget that I was once lost is when I become the most judgmental. That is a trait that only pushes teens further and further away from us.

Instead of being so judgmental, show that sense of kindness and concern that lets your teen know you want to walk with them through the challenges they face. They are yearning for that kind of compassion.

This service that you perform is not only supplying
the needs of the Lord's people but is also
overflowing in many expressions of thanks to God.

2 CORINTHIANS 9:12

Resolving the challenges that you face with your teen isn't just about overcoming issues so that you can have a peaceful home here and now. Working through the issues your teens faces will change the direction of their future. It will change the atmosphere of your family. It will affect who they pick as a future spouse. It will determine how they will raise your future grandkids. What you do now will gave a great effect on how they will live in the days ahead. Don't throw away this opportunity to change your family's destiny. Your persistence will eventually break through, and you will be thankful that you remained involved.

OCTOBER 22

The only thing that counts is faith
expressing itself through love.

GALATIANS 5:6

I've said it a million times: if all that we have learned in our relationship with Christ doesn't move us to love Him more and to love others in ways that are not humanly possible, then I'm not sure we've really grabbed hold of the essence of the gospel.

Given enough time, unconditional love can melt the coldest of hearts. And that love, which flows from the new person we've become in Christ, is like none other. It will embody grace and forgiveness. It will move toward those who offend us, motivate us to give, persuade us to overlook the harm inflicted by others, and impel us to offer more and more of ourselves to the point of sacrifice.

God so loved the world that He gave. Our giving should be reflected in how and with whom we share our treasures. That is a reflection of where our heart really is.

> *For the entire law is fulfilled in keeping this one*
> *command: "Love your neighbor as yourself."*
>
> GALATIANS 5:14

If I could be half the person my dog thinks I am, I'm sure I would be twice as well off. My dog listens, follows me, gets excited when she sees me, makes me laugh, doesn't say much, rests in my presence, is with me always, and never seems to get angry with me. She does what we ask of her. She's affectionate and loves being in our presence, and she never has a bad word to say about anyone else.

How I wish I could be that to my friends and neighbors.

The problem is that I am often thinking of myself first. If there is a day that I'm not thinking about myself for more than five minutes, that's a good day for me.

If I could think of others as much as I think about myself, I'm sure my relationships would be deeper and people would perhaps experience from me what I've experienced from my dog.

*Train yourself to be godly. For physical training is
of some value, but godliness has value for all things.*

1 TIMOTHY 4:7–8

*B*eing godly is not being godlike. It is taking on the
attributes of God in the life that He has given to me,
treating others as He has treated me, comforting others as
He has comforted me, being close to the brokenhearted as
He was to me when my heart was broken. Godliness has
more to do with the inward condition of the heart than
with outward appearances.

Lord, search my heart and see if there are any hurtful
ways lingering that I don't even know about. Show them to
me and lead me in a way where people see more of my heart
and less of my appearance.

> *The LORD blessed the latter part of Job's life*
> *more than the former part. He had fourteen*
> *thousand sheep, six thousand camels, a thousand*
> *yoke of oxen and a thousand donkeys.*

JOB 42:12

Just because everything isn't going well right now doesn't mean things can't change for the better later. For many families, having tunnel vision about the present stifles hope and exacerbates the frustrations they're currently facing.

Today's challenges will not go on forever. Our light and momentary troubles are achieving for us an eternal glory that far outweighs them all. At some point, resolution will happen. The current problem will be taken over by another problem. Once we learn one lesson, we move on to the next that the Lord has to teach us. It's just how He works.

On a side note, I'm not sure I would consider it a blessing to have fourteen thousand sheep, six thousand camels, one thousand oxen, and a thousand donkeys. To me, all of that would be a lot greater than some of the problems I've encountered in life.

*Get rid of all bitterness, rage and anger, brawling
and slander, along with every form of malice. Be
kind and compassionate to one another, forgiving
each other, just as in Christ God forgave you.*

EPHESIANS 4:31-32

*I*t's hard to move toward someone when they have done
you wrong. There is an innate, preprogrammed voice that
screams that we should stay away from danger and anything
that causes pain in our life. That self-preservation is a great
strategy when you're thinking about yourself, but it's not
such a good approach when you're thinking of others.

Offering grace to one who has offended you is the
hardest thing in the world because it compels you to do
the very thing that your programming says not to. Grace
moves toward the one who has offended and offers the
olive branch of relationship.

Likewise, if you have offended someone, their programming is telling them to keep their distance from you. It's hard
to be loving to people when they don't feel like loving you
back, but it's essential if restoration is going to take place.

Grace calls you to defy your programming, work to
restore what once was, and not allow small disputes to
divide the relationship God has called you to be in.

Brothers and sisters, I do not consider myself yet to have taken hold of it. But one thing I do: Forgetting what is behind and straining toward what is ahead.

PHILIPPIANS 3:13

*F*orgiving someone for the wrong they've committed against you is one thing; forgetting the impact of trauma and hurt is another. Quite honestly, I don't think anyone is capable of totally forgetting. What we are all able to do is make sure that those things from the past don't continue to haunt us. That's where some good counseling is essential to make sure you are properly working through the issues and are not under the control of the past.

One of the fruits of the Spirit is self-control, which is basically not letting anything that has happened to you control the way you feel or act toward other people. I'd encourage you to consider those challenges that have taken control of how your family operates. After you've considered how this has affected your family, work hard to not let forgivable situations determine the destiny of your life with your spouse and kids.

When you can't forget something that you have forgiven, choose not to dwell on something that cannot change; instead, make the decision to move to a place where you are not being controlled by it.

*But I said, "I have labored in vain; I have spent my
strength for nothing at all. Yet what is due me is in
the LORD's hand, and my reward is with my God."*

ISAIAH 49:4

How can something you did well go so wrong? It's a question that parents ask themselves all the time when they see their son or daughter start to spin out of control during their teen years. Parents then feel that all their work with the teen has gone to waste, and they experience a sense of doom and gloom in their relationships with others.

Let me assure you of something: all your work is not in vain. All the seeds that you have sown will come to fruition. All the time you've invested will not come back void. All the effort you've given is not wasted. The relationship you had will one day be restored.

When? We have no way of knowing. But we do know this: if you are doing what God wants you to do with that teen in your family, then you are not wasting your time. Don't grow weary, my friend.

*Flee the evil desires of youth and pursue
righteousness, faith, love and peace, along with
those who call on the Lord out of a pure heart.*

2 TIMOTHY 2:22

The chances are extremely high that your teens will be around, be offered, and might even partake of alcohol or other substances. The question is not if it happens what will I do, but when it happens what will I do?

I know six kids who have died of an overdose this past year. I don't think any of them really thought they were going to die, let alone wanted to. But they did. Their drug use, in a culture that is permissive and a pressure cooker for many, can be a family's worst nightmare.

So here are a couple of things that I would encourage. Have those discussions about "use," and start them long before they reach their adolescent years. The second encouragement is to set the example. Be the parent who doesn't allow your freedom to get in the way of your teen's acceptance of responsibility.

*"I will give them an undivided heart and put a
new spirit in them; I will remove from them their
heart of stone and give them a heart of flesh."*

EZEKIEL 11:19

Smart phones aren't going anywhere. The enticement of entertainment isn't going to diminish. The connection that happens through social networking sites isn't going away. And your teen's ability to balance it all has got to be developed through the encouragement, boundaries, and age-appropriate limits you establish so they can learn to integrate these devices and diversions into their life without being consumed by them.

It's important for you to come up with alternative forms of entertainment to the ones that are constantly enticing your teen to be looking at a screen. It's equally important that you give them a taste of what a real relationship looks like, and that will happen only through the time you pour into their life. Place reasonable limits, offer alternatives, and dig into the deeper areas of their life that will make them want to spend more time with you and less time on a phone.

It teaches us to say "No" to ungodliness and
worldly passions, and to live self-controlled,
upright and godly lives in this present age.

TITUS 2:12

All your teen's actions are motivated by the belief that something in their life is needed, missing, lost, or has been taken away. Their behavior is a visible expression of the invisible issues in their life, and some of those issues may be causing them to isolate. The greatest need your teen has is not for you to get more involved but for you to determine what is pushing the behavior that you see. They do what they do for a reason. The smart parent spends more time trying to find that reason rather than just changing their child's behavior.

Find out why they're disengaging. They may be scared to death, and your encouragement to get back out there may just be scaring them more, putting you in an awful position as a parent. Instead, offer your help, commit your time, and engage on a deeper level by asking questions that show your real concern and offering hope to a teen that may feel hopeless.

"Let the little children come to me, and do not hinder them, for the kingdom of heaven belongs to such as these."

MATTHEW 19:14

Adoption is one of the most admirable acts a person can make. Many adoptions come with a set of unknowns that begin to reveal themselves when an adopted child reaches their teen years. That doesn't mean that something is wrong with the adoption; it means the parents have got to switch gears to accommodate the new needs of their adopted teen to help them through a difficult time.

While most adopted kids I know don't fully accept their adoptions until their twenties, there's still hope to be a part of a teen's life as they seek the answers to the new questions that arise when they become an adolescent. The wise parent understands that nurture doesn't solve everything.

If you're currently facing this kind of struggle, remember why you adopted this child into your family, and know that God's plan was to have them enter into your life as much as you entered into His.

Be completely humble and gentle;
be patient, bearing with one another in love.

EPHESIANS 4:2

I feel like I'm preaching to the choir when I remind you that teens are selfish. They're born that way, and the way we make our lives revolve around them when they are very young by pleasing, protecting, and providing for them affirms that idea. It's a wonderful way to live until you get to the teen years, when it is essential that your "little selfish one" learns the reality that they are not the center of the universe.

What was once cute is now foolish. And truth be told, if their foolishness continues, they will lead miserable lives. So it's important that all parents help break this pattern of selfishness and push their teens to selflessness as their view of the world changes and they mature into healthy adults.

My dear brothers and sisters, take note of this:
Everyone should be quick to listen,
slow to speak and slow to become angry.

JAMES 1:19

Your conversations with your teen are important opportunities that can open up their heart and deepen your relationship with them. It all begins with your ability to first listen and then respond in a way that encourages future conversations.

When having a discussion, don't correct. Don't tell them how to say something differently or say it better. Don't tell them—show them. Don't just tell them how to have a conversation; become that conversation partner they long for, and I assure you they will come back for more.

In a world where no one listens, be the one who always gives an ear to your teen. Be slow to anger and slow to speak, but be quick to listen!

The righteous choose their friends carefully.

PROVERBS 12:26

The current generation of parents is faced with a new and interesting challenge: how to help their teens manage an opportunity to connect and help them understand how some aspects of social networking can negatively affect their life. Teens want to connect, and they want to be praised for their accomplishments. They want to be listened to and want someone to show an interest in their life. Knowing that they can find that online, you must determine how you will provide engagement offline that will meet their needs in a way that social networking cannot.

Here are a couple of things to accept: accept that social networking isn't going away and that your teen needs to engage with peers. Here's another challenge: Will you accept the role of being the one who will offer them what they're really searching for?

*Therefore confess your sins to each other
and pray for each other so that you may
be healed. The prayer of a righteous
person is powerful and effective.*

JAMES 5:16

Your teen wants to be heard. And there is no better person who can communicate a sense of value to your teen than you when you listen to their heart, process what they're saying, and respond with a great sense of wisdom... if you should respond at all.

If your teen delights in sharing his opinion, then quit sharing yours and listen to him.

If your teen needs to be heard when she speaks, then shut your mouth and open your ears.

Restrain your words, and be a parent of understanding.

Make your ear attentive, and incline your heart to understanding. You may just surprise your teen with your willingness to hear and listen to their comments.

Everyone wants to be heard... very few are wise enough to listen.

Do not forsake wisdom, and she will protect you;
love her, and she will watch over you.
The beginning of wisdom is this: Get wisdom.
Though it cost all you have, get understanding.

PROVERBS 4:6–7

Teens are drowning in information but are parched for wisdom. The search for an understanding ear is a teen's never-ending quest to find someone who will truly hear them and empathize with their plight.

Moms, dads, and grandparents, you can spend all your life gathering wisdom and understanding others, but if you never act on and personify those qualities, you won't be significant in the life of your teen.

The key to applying all that you have learned through your observation, reflection, and experience is to engage in a humble way that is agreeable to your teen and makes them want to follow your example.

We are never more of an example of Christ than when we become what Jesus described Himself to be—gentle and humble.

Don't let anyone look down on you because you are young, but set an example for the believers in speech, in conduct, in love, in faith and in purity.

1 TIMOTHY 4:12

The Internet has been a great thing for many. The speed of life has changed, information access has increased, and exposure to just about everything has entered the lives of our teens.

However it is something that we should train our teens to use. We should take the time to show them how to take full responsibility with how they spend their time on it, how they interact with the content on it, and how they communicate with others through it.

The example you set will make all the difference. If you're consumed, they will be. If you find your value online, they will. If you are pre-occupied with others, then so will your teens be. If you don't give your teens the "value" they need, they will find it elsewhere.

Set some boundaries, have those ongoing discussions, and don't be afraid to set some limits on their use of their phone and the Internet. You are the one who will set the stage for your teens.

*"And whoever welcomes one such child
in my name welcomes me."*

MATTHEW 18:5

Have you ever thought that, maybe, just maybe, those questionable kids who have been placed in your teen's life might have been placed there by God Himself because He wants you to play a redemptive role in their lives?

Maybe your mission field is those teens who you'd prefer your teens not hang out with, for He wants to use you to offer something to them that they'll never get anywhere else.

You don't have to travel to a distant country to help the lost. They may be right in your backyard, and God has placed them in your life for a reason.

I often wonder if "bad kids" were welcomed into the homes of great parents if it would change their destinies and teach parents some wonderful lessons of how to take their faith and be His example of love to those who are unlovely around them.

"The King will reply, 'Truly I tell you, whatever you did for one of the least of these brothers and sisters of mine, you did for me.'"

MATTHEW 25:40

Your acts of kindness and generosity will never be more noticed by our Lord than when those acts are done without recognition, payment, or wanting anything in return.

We've been blessed. And if you think about it, we've been blessed far more than we deserve. The recognition of that blessing should motivate us all to be to others who He is us. A blessing!

Give it a shot. Pick someone around you who would be encouraged and blessed by your involvement in his or her life. The time you spend doing anything extra to help people is not a sacrifice; it's an honor to offer the same to others as what God has offered you.

Think of ways that you can make the Word become flesh in the life of just one person around you today without hope that someone will see you. When you do that, you will know that what you did for Him has given that person a taste of the character of God.

*Get rid of all bitterness, rage and anger, brawling
and slander, along with every form of malice.*

EPHESIANS 4:31

*L*et me tell you a story that is a reminder of God's
continual working in our lives.

I've always been angry at my dad for all the things he
didn't "bring to the table" in my life. I was disappointed that
he had no interest in me, didn't connect in any way, and
was always somewhat distant. And these disappointments
showed through countless actions where I felt his rejection.

One night I dreamed I died and went to heaven. As I
approached God's throne, I saw my Dad standing next to
God. I asked, "What is he doing here?"

God looked at me, pointed His finger, and said, "I want
you to know that I've been using this man to create in you
the person I've wanted you to be."

From that day forward, I've never felt a sense of anger
toward my Dad. With just one sentence from God, I was
able to put away all the bitterness and rage I had carried for
years, knowing that God was at work in me and had used
my Dad to mold me.

What anger are you holding onto where you've been
wronged? Have you thought that God may have placed that
"wrong thing" in your life for a reason?

Just as a nursing mother cares for her children,
so we cared for you. Because we loved you so
much, we were delighted to share with you not
only the gospel of God but our lives as well.

1 THESSALONIANS 2:7–8

What speaks louder than words? Actions! For it is your actions that prove your words. And if there's ever a time that teens need to see genuine and godly men and women, it is now, simply because those examples are few and far between.

It's not what you say; it's who you are. It's not your words; it's your actions. The actions of your heart put feet to the words of your mouth. It's the example of your life that brings life to the words of Scripture. The proof of the voice your teen hears is seen through the actions of your life, which gives a living example of a man or woman of integrity.

It's your time to prove to your teens that living a godly and pure life is not just words to live by. It is a life that is filled with love, patience, kindness, and empathy . . . just the kind of love that God has for each one of us.

Fathers, do not embitter your children,
or they will become discouraged.

COLOSSIANS 3:21

*T*eens are looking for a sense of relief from the pressures of their everyday life, and if they can't find rest for their embattled souls at home, they'll find it elsewhere. If teens don't have a safe haven from their contrary adolescent culture, they may be on a path to violating the principles they've been taught their whole lives.

You've got to counter the pressures of this culture by creating a home that is calmer than the world in which your teen exists. Can you let up on some rules? Can you loosen up on some restrictions? Can you look at your own life and determine if you're adding to the pressure? These are important questions for wise parents to ask about their homes.

*Whatever happens, conduct yourselves in a
manner worthy of the gospel of Christ. Then,
whether I come and see you or only hear
about you in my absence, I will know that
you stand firm in the one Spirit, striving
together as one for the faith of the gospel.*

PHILIPPIANS 1:27

Your teen wants to be prepared for the world they're about to enter. That means you have to be intentional about allowing them to experience life at a level that exposes them to the reality of their culture, while also protecting them from making life-changing decisions that would negatively alter the course of their destiny. It's a delicate balance of permitting them to make decisions while not letting them be totally on their own.

So set a plan that will let them assume more responsibility, make more decisions, and handle more freedom so that you'll have the opportunity to speak truth into their life when decisions could have been better, when freedom might have been used more wisely, and when they weren't as responsible as they should have been.

Whoever conceals their sins does not prosper, but the one who confesses and renounces them finds mercy.

PROVERBS 28:13

Trust is something your teen is responsible for showing you. It's not your role to figure out how to trust them; it's their responsibility to show you that they can be trusted.

Trust isn't necessarily built on a mistake-free life. It forms in an atmosphere that allows teens to share their mistakes and blunders when they blow it or don't live up to the expectations you have for them. And if they can admit their mistakes, what a great opportunity to share your wisdom and train them not to make the same mistake twice.

Show them the benefits of confession by admitting your own mistakes, by sharing when you "blew it" and made wrong decisions. That atmosphere will create an opening for them to listen to your wise counsel and for you to affirm your love for them when they've made mistakes.

"Never will I leave you; never will I forsake you."

HEBREWS 13:5

Your teen really does want a relationship with you. They don't want to lose something that has been dear to their heart. In all my years, I've never met a teen who has said, "I'd really love to hate my parents when I'm thirty." I've never heard a teen say that they would love to never see their parents again. And I've never heard a teen say they didn't want to have a relationship with their mom or dad.

It's your responsibility to remain engaged and shift your parenting style to accommodate the changing needs of your adolescent teen. Your mindset must be intentional in the pursuit of your teen. Do what is necessary to remain a valued part of their lives—your teen desperately wants you to do that.

To the arrogant I say, "Boast no more,"
and to the wicked, "Do not lift up your horns."

PSALM 75:4

Teens are moving from being totally selfish to learning about being selfless over the course of their adolescent years. It's more of a marathon than a sprint, so adjust your expectations accordingly, and give them time to work through this process.

In your parenting toolbox should be strategies to help them break their selfish nature and learn that it's better to give than receive and to count others as more important than themselves.

The best lesson will be your example. You will show them the reward and significance of a selfless life and the satisfaction that comes from emulating the humble servanthood of our Savior.

Surely you remember, brothers and sisters, our toil and hardship; we worked night and day in order not to be a burden to anyone while we preached the gospel of God to you. You are witnesses, and so is God, of how holy, righteous and blameless we were among you who believed. For you know that we dealt with each of you as a father deals with his own children, encouraging, comforting and urging you to live lives worthy of God, who calls you into his kingdom and glory.

1 THESSALONIANS 2:9–12

Chances are your child will become lost during their teen years. And there's an even greater chance that they will experience a loss during that time: the death of a dog, losing a grandparent, the breakup of a relationship, or not attaining something they really wanted or hoped for. How you engage with your teen during their times of loss or loneliness will determine whether they lose their way. This isn't a time for "I told you so" or a time to harp on them for making bad decisions. It's a time to wrap your arms around them and let them know you'll always be present when they feel alone and that you'll hear anything they have to say. It's an important time for your relationship, and your response might just keep them off a path they never really wanted to walk on.

Dear children, let us not love with words
or speech but with actions and in truth.

1 JOHN 3:18

Here's a quick list to engaging with your teen: let them be the smartest person in the room for a change, eliminate the lectures, pick your battles wisely, loosen up on some of the rules as they get older, ask questions that go somewhere, respect their need for privacy, spend time together doing something they want to do, know their world, lighten up a bit, treat them like an adult, and spend more time listening than talking.

Quite a list, eh? It will work only if you truly have more interest in the condition of their heart than the condition of their room or how good their grades are. Your genuinely selfless mindset will set the stage for them to be able to engage with you and have those conversations you long to have.

Your conversation has more to do with the atmosphere you create than with the words you speak.

Yes, my soul, find rest in God; my hope comes from him. Truly he is my rock and my salvation; he is my fortress, I will not be shaken. My salvation and my honor depend on God; he is my mighty rock, my refuge. Trust in him at all times, you people; pour out your hearts to him, for God is our refuge.

PSALM 62:5–8

Your teens live in an intense culture of comparison, criticism, competitiveness, and confusion. So you must create a place of peace for your teen at home, or you will have to deal with their inappropriate behaviors as they try to find relief elsewhere.

Jesus meant what He said about coming to Him for rest. It's a picture of what it means to be close to the heart of God when you create a home that is a place of safety and comfort, one of encouragement and hope, and one that entices your child to let their hair down in your presence. You need that place, and so does your teen.

Cast all your anxiety on him
because he cares for you.

1 PETER 5:7

*D*epression is real. Our teens are masters at performing as if nothing is wrong, and they are careful to hide feelings of imperfection—those times when they feel they don't measure up to the images and messages that bombard them through social media. They are dogged continually and live in a culture that presents challenges and questions about how you've been raising your teens. When teens feel like they don't have the answers, can't overcome those challenges, or struggle to be who they have been raised to be, it can be a depressing time. That's when you've got to be on your guard to remain connected with your teen so you can pick up on any signs of depression or hopelessness.

Communicate daily, encourage constantly, and become a student of your teen, asking about their feelings and thoughts, and showing more concern for their mental health than their academic and sporting pursuits. Just as the Lord is close to the brokenhearted, so must you be also. It might just make all the difference in the world to your teen.

*Though I walk in the midst of trouble, you preserve
my life. You stretch out your hand against the anger
of my foes; with your right hand you save me.*

PSALMS 138:7

Old-school bullying was usually a one-on-one interaction. Not so today. Nowadays bullying often happens online, and hundreds may be witness to the shaming of and critical remarks hurled at innocent and wonderful teens. Your teen could easily be a target of someone's anger and ridicule.

It's important for you to keep your finger on the pulse of your teen's emotional health and to remain connected so you can recognize any shift in their attitude, mindset, and demeanor and help them through a difficult time.

The shaming that comes with bullying often carries with it damage that can last a lifetime. So do whatever you need to do to prevent it, manage it, and correct its affects. Approach the bully with strength while being kind, tenderhearted, and forgiving, just as God in Christ forgave you.

> *My brothers and sisters, if one of you should*
> *wander from the truth and someone should bring*
> *that person back, remember this: Whoever turns*
> *a sinner from the error of their way will save them*
> *from death and cover over a multitude of sins.*

JAMES 5:19–20

Your teen wants to belong somewhere. And they will stop at nothing—good or bad—to achieve that. A keen awareness of your teen's driving motivation will help you understand the actions you see them choosing. For example, when your teen spends way too much time on their phone, at the core of their behavior is a longing to find a place of belonging and a desire to maintain their place in the hierarchy of their culture.

Many times, a teen will forfeit belonging to God for the sake of belonging to a group of peers. This is usually a temporary distraction from the significance they find in a relationship with their Lord. In time, given the opportunity for a welcomed return, they'll come back to the One who created them with this desire for relationship, especially the one they have with Him.

As a door turns on its hinges,
so a sluggard turns on his bed.

PROVERBS 26:14

Grades are important, but they're not as important as you might think. What's really important is your teen's acceptance of responsibility for their grades. If you're the one doing all the pushing and pulling to get them to do homework, complete assignments, and study their subjects, then you might just be the one who is keeping them from becoming responsible for their academic performance.

Let me ask you a question: Which is more important, grades or your relationship with your teen? Your relationship is, of course! So, when they're sixteen years old, let them know that they are responsible for their grades and will also be the recipient of any consequences for not completing their academic requirements. It's hard to see your teen flunk a class. But it's a lesson well learned if that failure drives them to take initiative in the future.

Let your conversation be always full of
grace, seasoned with salt, so that you
may know how to answer everyone.

COLOSSIANS 4:6

All teens struggle in some form or fashion. The issue becomes if the struggle controls their life and becomes their motivation for inappropriate behavior. Usually that struggle revolves around taking what they know to be true and trying to apply it in a world that is sometimes contrary to what they've been taught. Rarely, if ever, do I meet teens who want to be mean. Never do I meet teens who strive to be out of control. They all want to have it together; they just don't know how. Your teen might not be rebellious. Chances are they're just lost.

The answer is to help them when they need you the most. It's called grace—something every teen needs now and then.

*Show me, LORD, my life's end and the number of
my days; let me know how fleeting my life is.
You have made my days a mere handbreadth; the
span of my years is as nothing before you. Everyone
is but a breath, even those who seem secure.*

PSALM 39:4–5

Your teen wants to make choices along the path that you have set for them. Sound familiar? Man plans his steps, but God directs his path. In the same way, let your teen make choices along the path that you have set before them—a path that leads to where they feel they want to go. That doesn't mean you help your teen crash and burn if they choose a path of destruction, but your teen does need to be involved in charting their own course. That usually happens in a series of discussions and not in a onetime ten-minute chat. It takes time. But the time you take to put together a path will be well worth the investment as you see your teen making progress toward a great place.

Give thanks to the LORD, for he is
good; his love endures forever.

PSALM 118:1

Gratitude is a character trait displayed by those who recognize they are owed nothing yet are accepting of others' involvement in their life. Many times we become so concerned with collecting and getting more that we forget to be thankful for what we have.

I wonder at times if my ungratefulness has produced a sense of entitlement in the lives of my family members. Perhaps I should be concerned less about bemoaning others' entitlement and focus more on helping those in my family to be a little more grateful for what they have, reminding them all of when we didn't have anything.

God has provided for all our material needs, and for that I am grateful. But I'm most grateful for the love that I'm not entitled to, the love He freely gives.

*The heart is deceitful above all things and
beyond cure. Who can understand it?*

JEREMIAH 17:9

*B*eing rejected by someone who lives in your own home is tough. It's probably one of the hardest times for a mom or dad when their teen rejects them. But let me assure you that this is more than likely just a temporary phase that will soon pass if you take advantage of the time and make sure that you are not the one who is causing the alienation.

Your teen wants to have closeness with you. And if you can't change them, then you have to figure out ways to change yourself and consider the possibility that you may be the cause of the strain in the relationship. Ask others about the way you engage, ask your teen what they would love to see changed in your family, and be honest about any bad habits that you recognize in your life. Your willingness to make changes will set an example for your teen to do the same.

*By wisdom a house is built, and through
understanding it is established; through knowledge
its rooms are filled with rare and beautiful treasures.*

PROVERBS 24:3-4

Communication among teens has changed drastically. Information bombards their minds, but wisdom eludes their hearts. Comparison with others replaces the confidence they had as younger children. The demand for perfection creates a world of anxiety and depression. And it's a world where everyone is more intentional about spouting their own opinions rather than listening to anyone else's heart. It's a tough culture.

You can help by setting some boundaries for younger teens, giving more freedom to older ones, and asking all to be responsible. Your teens don't need your information; they need your wisdom about relationships, and they need you to create for them a place of rest. Jesus said, "Come to me, all who are weary and burdened, and I will give you rest." Your home should be that place where your teen can refresh, restore, and be prepared to face the challenges of their culture.

Honor your father and your mother, so
that you may live long in the land the
LORD your God is giving you.

EXODUS 20:12

Your teen lives in a world of disrespect, self-contempt, and apathy. It's bound to rub off on them once in a while. It's reflected in the way they perceive authority, the way they succumb to entitlement, and the way they engage in relationships. It's important that you be the one who gently asks for and occasionally demands respect in a world of insolence.

The old-style approach of requiring respect through an authoritarian approach just doesn't work the way it used to. Your respectful approach will, in return, produce a respectful response. You still have the authority that God gave you as a parent. It's just important that you use it in a way that's going to be productive. I'm not saying that you tolerate insult and ridicule, but I am saying that you understand the reasons behind their actions and approach their disrespect in a way that helps them understand that respect is a key element in their pursuit of relationships.

*A good man brings good things out of the
good stored up in him, and an evil man brings
evil things out of the evil stored up in him.*

MATTHEW 12:35

As a parent, you will be the greatest influence in the life of your teen and the best teacher in helping them learn what relationships look like with their peers. The relationship equation includes respect, engagement, kindness, and selflessness, with a whole lot of listening and compassion. It's more about the life you live than the words you speak, more about the example you show than the lessons you teach. Moms and dads, you are a light amid the darkness, an anchor that holds fast, and a caring rock that has your teen's back when they are in need.

*The Word became flesh and made
his dwelling among us.*

JOHN 1:14

You have a chance to start over in the pursuit of a renewed relationship with your teen in a few weeks. Sometimes relationships need an overhaul, a fresh coat of paint, or some correction to neglected maintenance issues. Do you hear what I'm saying? Your teen would love to have some new chances, and I'm sure there are some things you would like to see different. Are you waiting for them to ask you? This is where you'll need to step up and have that hard conversation about what you'd like to see different and how you're going to make those changes that usher in a new year. God will use you in a mighty way to give your teen a taste of His character.

Jesus wept.
JOHN 11:35

*F*unerals have always been hard for me. It's not just that I'm going to miss the person who has passed or because I'm uncertain about the hereafter. They are hard because there are times that I feel I'm going to lose it and fall apart. I strive hard to deflect my emotions and do everything I can to make sure I don't end up becoming a snot-dripping, sobbing mess. It's almost as if I'm more concerned about my appearance than sharing my grief over the loss of someone dear. How fake is that?

I was taught that a man should never fall apart, that we're always to have it together. Don't cry. Don't flinch. Don't let anyone know you are hurting.

If I hold to that teaching, I will sadly pass on the same disingenuous habits to those around me.

Those two words, "Jesus wept," give me permission to be authentic in front of all who know me. That encouragement teaches others that it's okay not to have it all together, that it's all right to hurt, to struggle, and to be disheveled. It is then that relationships will grow deeper, and other people will feel permission to struggle in my presence.

The LORD delights in those who fear him,
who put their hope in his unfailing love.

PSALM 147:11

*O*nce a child reaches middle school, parents start to fade out of the social picture, and kids are supposed to start making their own plans, keeping up with sophisticatedly rude discussions, and being able to go out on their own without supervision. It's that hard time as a parent when you have to begin to let go and watch the pain and reality of life creep into your child's world—and your kids are scared to death.

Never has there been a time when they need you more—but not in the same way that they've needed you in the past.

They need a place of rest. They need a little encouragement. And they need a person who helps them realize that these times will pass and aren't the best days of their lives. They need hope.

The LORD detests lying lips, but he
delights in people who are trustworthy.

PROVERBS 12:22

Teens lie for a reason. It may be to get out of a consequence, which is a pretty normal response to getting caught. Or it may be that they fear losing a relationship with you should you learn the truth. Or they're covering up something they're ashamed of and would like for you to know that truth. Or they just plain don't want to let you down.

This is where affirming your commitment to loving them unconditionally is a message of hope. This lets them know that you are a safe place and are strong enough to hear whatever they have to say. Discourage the lies but encourage the truth; this allows the relationship to deepen while your teen experiences the consequences of their behavior.

Anxiety weighs down the heart,
but a kind word cheers it up.

PROVERBS 12:25

*T*eens get depressed about what they are unsure of. Anxiety is worry that leads to fear and panic of the unknown. It is a great motivator in small doses, such as feeling nervous about completing an assignment, speaking in front of others, and being able to perform in a certain way. But in larger doses, it can overwhelm the heart of a teen, shutting them down to the point that getting out of bed is a difficult task.

Helping your child through bouts of the larger doses of anxiety may take a lot of listening, the advice of a counselor, medication, and assurances from you that the wall they think they're facing isn't nearly as big as they think it is. You can help your teen through these anxious years, but don't ignore the signs of this mindset that can become crippling and turn into something darker and much more dangerous.

*Only be careful, and watch yourselves closely
so that you do not forget the things your
eyes have seen or let them fade from your
heart as long as you live. Teach them to your
children and to their children after them.*

DEUTERONOMY 4:9

Grandparents, you can play a very special role in your teen's life if you are intentional about that engagement, are willing to shift your stye to remain relevant, and are willing to accommodate your grandchild during a time when they are experiencing so much change. Your teen wants to maintain the relationship that you had with them during their preteen years, and parents also want you involved in their life. But not as another set of parents. They need a deep relationship with you that is full of wisdom and acceptance.

The shortest distance between two people is a story, and it is your stories of how you've navigated life that will become a compass to your grandkids long after you're gone. So start sharing and let the rivers of wisdom flow!

The Lord is not slow in keeping his promise,
as some understand slowness. Instead he
is patient with you, not wanting anyone to
perish, but everyone to come to repentance.

2 PETER 3:9

I'm never surprised when I find out about a teen who is using drugs. I've seen every type of teen from every walk of life get caught in the web of illicit substances. It usually starts out with curiosity and stems from a desire to self-medicate or to use recreationally, but they end up flirting with death. The same world that has created a culture of anxiety and depression has also produced, promoted, and given permission for teens to experiment, which usually leads to a bad place. The path of drugs will cause your teen to lose motivation, hate what they once loved, and eventually fall flat on their face.

With this in mind, the first line of defense is believing that your teen is capable of choosing this lifestyle. Don't think they never will, because they just might. Encourage your teens that there is hope and that life does get better, but it will only get worse if they choose a path that is destructive and deadly.

We are hard pressed on every side, but not crushed;
perplexed, but not in despair; persecuted, but
not abandoned; struck down, but not destroyed.

2 CORINTHIANS 4:8–9

When your teen begins to wrestle with what they've been taught, you have an amazing opportunity to help them transition from their immature faith into a deeper and more fulfilling relationship with Christ. As they encounter new challenges to their faith and are exposed to new ways of life and differing opinions and viewpoints, their questioning is really a sign of growth.

Take advantage of this time. Have those tough discussions. Admit where you might be confused about Scripture. Share your past struggles. Encourage your child to continue to question all they've learned in a way that produces growth, not in a way that pushes them away from God. Your teen will find the answers they seek when they seek Him with all their heart and strive to apply His answers to the new questions around them.

Carry each other's burdens.

GALATIANS 6:2

*L*oss is tough. The recognition that something that once was is no longer is hard. The loss of a loved one, be it animal or person, ushers in a feeling of aloneness. And having something taken away is not always an easy pill to swallow.

I'm convinced of this: The only way to process those losses in our lives is to talk about them, to have conversations that allow us to express our feelings and emotions. They are best had when in the presence of someone who genuinely cares about what we're going through. Loss, in one sense, connects us with those who care the most about us.

Talk about those things that you are unsure of. About those unfulfilled losses that still linger. About losses that still hurt, and even today, feel like they'll never be filled. It is only then that one can feel comfortable about sharing their hurts and pains. Your teens need your caring and listening ear.

*Resist him, standing firm in the faith, because you
know that the family of believers throughout the world
is undergoing the same kind of sufferings. And the
God of all grace, who called you to his eternal glory in
Christ, after you have suffered a little while, will himself
restore you and make you strong, firm and steadfast.*

1 PETER 5:9–10

The message that every parent should be sharing with
their teens is that their teen years are not the best
years of their life. Every mom and dad and grandparent
should be spending more time giving perspectives of life to
their teens than sharing opinions.

Your discussions about the temporary struggles they are
facing can usher in a sense of hope that your teen will know
that their temporary struggles will soon pass. It's through
your sharing of mistakes, difficulties, challenges, and struggles, coupled with the way that you've gotten through them
all, that will let them know that what they face will soon
pass, and they will be stronger, more firm, and restored to
face the challenges of the future.

It's imparting real-life with real solutions that let them
know they are not alone but surrounded by loving relationships that are committed to suffer with them through their
struggles.

Whatever is true ... noble ... right ... pure ...
lovely ... admirable—if anything is excellent or
praiseworthy—think about such things.

PHILIPPIANS 4:8

I always wonder if I've done all my work as unto the Lord. Have I been the spouse that God desires me to be? Have I offered myself to others selflessly? Do I have a deeper relationship with my kids this year than in years past? It's kind of a self-reflective report card. All good questions that never fail to encourage me to do more and to applaud my areas of accomplishment.

It's also a time that I celebrate those accomplishments. Not in a party kind of way, but more so with internal "pats on the back" that only I know about. I do that not by giving myself gifts but by giving others a bit of what I have, knowing that all I have is from Him.

What about you? Is this a time of reflection? Why don't you take a little time to just look at the past twelve months. Make changes in your lifestyle where needed and celebrate your successes. I guarantee you'll see God's hand in it all.

He said: "In my distress I called to the LORD, and
he answered me. From deep in the realm of the
dead I called for help, and you listened to my cry."

JONAH 2:2

There are times that parents feel alone, especially when a family member is struggling to keep their head above water and drowning their ability to see anything good in their life. If you ever get to this "drowning point," don't hesitate to cry out! Ask for help. Search for answers. And reach out to those trusted friends and colleagues who can offer comfort and throw you that lifeline in your time of need.

Don't isolate. God never intended for you to go through struggles and hardships in your family as a loner. Speak to someone. Get their insight and wisdom. Hear their comforting words. And embrace their words of encouragement. God has put these people in your life for a reason.

For in the day of trouble he will keep me safe
in his dwelling; he will hide me in the shelter of
his sacred tent and set me high upon a rock.

PSALM 27:5

Anxiety is on the rise, and depression is evident in the lives of teens everywhere. Social avoidance is one way your teen tries to eliminate the fears they feel about their interactions, whether it be with you or with their circle of friends. Their isolation is rooted in fear, stimulated by their need to be in control, and fueled by worry of what it would take to interact with the culture they are most fearful of.

You can help break that pattern of isolation. Create safe places in your home where they can rest and find comfort outside of their bedroom. Gently remind them that worry is a misuse of their imagination and can quickly lead to anxiety and panic. Spend time one on one discussing how you might be able to help. Break their isolation by your involvement, and move toward them, even when they want to move away from you.

"If anyone causes one of these little ones—those who believe in me—to stumble, it would be better for them if a large millstone were hung around their neck and they were thrown into the sea."

MARK 9:42

*D*ivorce is tough, especially on your kids. While blended families and split homes are prevalent, I've never met anyone who anticipated such a breakup. There's no judgment here, but I do want you to know that some teens are greatly affected by having a "two-Christmas" holiday or having to split their time between homes.

Create a stable and calm haven of rest, somewhere that can be counted on and remembered as a place of affirmation and encouragement. Be ready to listen to whatever is on your teen's heart. Making the most and striving for the best in the worst of situations is key, and communicating reassurance of your relationship will be a big part of that.

*And do not forget to do good and to share with
others, for with such sacrifices God is pleased.*

HEBREWS 13:16

The older your teen gets, the more you have to work at keeping the communication lines open. This is especially true for all you grandparents. As your teen's social circles enlarge, make sure you are not pushed out or replaced by someone or something else. They're distracted with exploring new avenues of their life. If you're not intentional about pursuing your relationship with them, it will soon become an image in the rearview mirror, growing smaller and smaller as they move forward.

Be intentional. Go and initiate a visit. Spend some time and some dollars doing things together. Make some more memories together, and reminisce about all the good times they've had with you. Let them know you still want to be a part of their life.

*That is why a man leaves his father and mother
and is united to his wife, and they become one flesh.*

GENESIS 2:24

*O*ne day you will celebrate the engagement of your
son or daughter to the one who will join your family
and hopefully produce some wonderful grandkids who
will bless you in ways you would have never imagined. It
all begins with a date, a get-together, where a spark signals
the beginning of a relationship that will change the destiny
of your family.

Don't be afraid, and don't keep the process from
happening. Just stay involved in your teen's life while they
date so you can speak truth into their life, have those hard
talks about love and sex, and give them direction when
confusion and doubt enter. Pray now that God will bring a
godly person into your teen's life, and pray for them whenever they start that dating process.

*You are witnesses, and so is God, of how holy, righteous
and blameless we were among you who believed.
For you know that we dealt with each of you as a
father deals with his own children, encouraging,
comforting and urging you to live lives worthy of
God, who calls you into his kingdom and glory.*

1 THESSALONIANS 2:10–12

Mark my words: one day you'll realize that you are having a very real and genuine discussion with your teen. It will come at a time when you least expect it, and I guarantee you'll walk away from that talk with a smile on your face.

It will happen as a result of spending time being that authentic person who is willing to encourage, exhort, and inspire them to walk in a manner that is worthy of our calling as Christians. They'll know how to have discussions because of the example you've set by listening to understand, asking questions to take them deeper, and not correcting their every thought.

They will remember how devout and upright you have been, and my prayer for you is that they will follow your example as you follow that of our Lord.

*Brothers and sisters, stop thinking like
children. In regard to evil be infants,
but in your thinking be adults.*

1 CORINTHIANS 14:20

*J*ust because a teen makes a mistake or chooses unwisely, it doesn't mean they're being rebellious. They might be trying to communicate a message through their actions, but few are intentionally mean and vile. Most are lost and are wandering through adolescence looking for answers to the questions bouncing around in their head.

If you detach when you think they are rebellious, you are losing your position in their life at a time when they really need you the most. Yes, their actions may disappoint you and even make you mad and make you want to walk away. But remember this: if we are to parent our children with the same patience and grace that God has shown to us, then we must walk toward them at a time we'd prefer to do otherwise. It is in those times that your teen will embrace the message of your unfailing love for them.

*In my distress I called to the Lord; I cried to my
God for help. From his temple he heard my voice.*

PSALM 18:6

Silence isn't always golden. Quietness sometimes speaks louder than a teen who screams to get what they want. Sometimes the quiet is peaceful, but it may just be the calm before the storm. When your teen shuts down, they may do so because they don't know what to say, how to express their feelings, or are ashamed that they don't know how to fix something in their life. They might just be embarrassed. So don't ignore the silence of your teen.

Some of your greatest communication can be made without words. Your presence can speak louder than any words. Don't disengage when you don't get a response. Just remain connected so that your teen will eventually be comfortable enough to express their feelings and feel that they will be heard loud and clear.

For just as we share abundantly in the sufferings of Christ, so also our comfort abounds through Christ.

2 CORINTHIANS 1:5

Our kids are growing up in a world that has a few more challenges than when you and I were their age. With those challenges comes an immense amount of pressure, and teens often don't know how to use healthy relief valves to calm the raging storm within themselves. Because drugs offer the promise of relief, the world offers them as a way of dealing with an intense culture. Don't ever think that your teen isn't susceptible to the influence and appeal of drugs, no matter what form they come in. No teen is immune from influence and popular appeal. Ask questions, watch their behavior, be smart, and pray for the challenges your teen faces. Create that resting place at home so they won't have to go finding relief elsewhere.

"Sanctify them by the truth; your word is truth."

JOHN 17:17

Scripture is truth, and that truth is not determined by my understanding or acceptance of it. There might even be times that you question, and perhaps even doubt, that God's Word is truth. The challenge for most of us it to take the Scripture as we know it and apply its principles and values to a culture where truth doesn't always fit. I believe Scripture when I'm sure about it. I believe Scripture when I'm not so sure. I may even believe Scripture when I have no earthly idea of how to practically apply it. The truth of Scripture is not determined by me.

Over time, I have come to understand that even when I'm not sure, Scripture will show itself in ways that affirm the commandments, encouragements, warnings and requirements are all God's attempt to love on me.

Cast your cares on the LORD and he will sustain you; he will never let the righteous be shaken.

PSALM 55:22

Christmas is a time of giving gifts to celebrate the great gift God has given us through His Son, Jesus. Do something different this Christmas: give your teen a gift they don't expect, or maybe hardly deserve. A gift of grace given at the right time can change the coldest of hearts.

Do something unexpected. Give something different. Make comments they've never heard before. Change it up. Laugh a little more. Spend more time this Christmas listening to their heart as they, too, reflect on the past twelve months and desire some "fresh starts" in the upcoming year. Merry Christmas, my friend. Enjoy this season of giving gifts!

*So Joseph also went up from the town of Nazareth
in Galilee to Judea, to Bethlehem the town of David,
because he belonged to the house and line of David. He
went there to register with Mary, who was pledged to
be married to him and was expecting a child. While
they were there, the time came for the baby to be
born, and she gave birth to her firstborn, a son. She
wrapped him in cloths and placed him in a manger,
because there was no guest room available for them.*

LUKE 2:4–7

My prayer for you and your family is that this Christmas week would be a blessed and happy time, regardless of any circumstance you find yourself in. My hope is that this time will be a restful one for you and your loved ones. I encourage you to celebrate in a way that you've never celebrated the Messiah's birth before. Have a special dinner. Go to a movie and laugh with your kids. Turn off the electricity to your house for a night, sit around the fireplace, and tell stories by candlelight. Do something memorable. Experience something magnificent, and make your time together meaningful. Merry Christmas!

Today in the town of David a Savior has been
born to you; he is the Messiah, the Lord. This
will be a sign to you: You will find a baby
wrapped in cloths and lying in a manger.

LUKE 2:11–12

Remember when you brought your child home for the first time? There was an excitement and joyous celebration for what God provided for your family. The preciousness of this new child was overwhelming. Just because you're going through a tough time with your teen doesn't mean that "God has left the building." Your teen is just as precious in His sight as the day you brought them home. God knew this child was going to need some special attention when they reached adolescence, and that's why He chose you to be their parent.

The crisis will be temporary, and the struggle will pass. In time, your teen will realize the beauty of having you as a parent as they process all the thoughts bouncing around in their head. So keep the relationship strong, even when you want to walk away, and know that God has not forgotten you or your family.

For to us a child is born, to us a son is given,
and the government will be on his shoulders.
And he will be called Wonderful Counselor, Mighty
God, Everlasting Father, Prince of Peace.

ISAIAH 9:6

*O*h, what a day this is! A day to celebrate the birth of the Christ child, the Savior of the world! As you pursue cooking meals, traveling, visiting family, and everything else that happens today, remember that these are not always the best of times for many. With that in mind, do what you can to create a space for others that is restful, refreshing, and full of hope.

Let your family not only hear about the goodness of God; let them also see His desire for us all to rest in His presence and enjoy this season of celebration. Merry Christmas, all! My prayer is that this will be a restful Christmas for you and yours.

Therefore, my dear brothers and sisters, stand firm. Let nothing move you. Always give yourselves fully to the work of the Lord, because you know that your labor in the Lord is not in vain.

1 CORINTHIANS 15:58

I f you have a teen who is spinning out of control, then you know the pain of watching a child violate everything they've been taught and the heartache of watching a once-happy child now become miserable. They're likely more lost than they are rebellious, and I'm convinced they're more miserable than you are.

But don't lose hope. All those seeds that you have sown into their life will come to fruition if you maintain the fertile soil of a relationship that encourages a plan for resolving conflict and growing in understanding and respect for one another. Now would be a great time to let your teen know that no matter what they do, your love for them and desire to have them as a part of your life will never change.

*I keep asking that the God of our Lord Jesus
Christ, the glorious Father, may give you
the Spirit of wisdom and revelation.*

EPHESIANS 1:17

It's about to be a new year! My prayer as you enter into this new year is that there will be something new for your family: a new direction, a new attitude, and a new commitment to deepen relationships within the circle of people God has placed you in. Every day is a new start, every new year a fresh opportunity to make those changes you've longed to make for a very long time.

Sit down with your family and share this new opportunity for you all to make some changes. Your kids will never follow if you don't lead in this area.

Happy New Year, my friend. I pray that this year will be one of blessings for you and yours!

"For I know the plans I have for you,"
declares the LORD, "plans to prosper you and not
to harm you, plans to give you hope and a future."

JEREMIAH 29:11

C. S. Lewis once said, "We are not necessarily doubting that God will do the best for us; we are wondering how painful the best will turn out to be."

Pain is tough. I don't know anyone who wants a pain-filled life. Yet embracing and enduring the pain that is placed before you provides a way for God to build a strong character in you that comes from persevering through these light and momentary troubles. Don't be defined by pain; instead, allow yourself and your child to grow in its presence. And rather than letting those tough, painful times ruin relationships, use them to deepen your love for one another.

"So the last will be first, and the first will be last."

MATTHEW 20:16

*S*elfishness comes so easily! We are all born with a selfish bent, but it's a parent's (and grandparent's) role to help our teens get out of it and become sensitive to the lives of others. It's moving them from getting up every morning asking, "What is everyone going to do for me today?" to "What am I going to do for someone else today?"

It all begins with you. Your teen will observe the example you set through the words you speak and the way you treat the people around you. In you they will see the example of a servant living life for the benefit of others, just like the servant's heart seen in Jesus—the one you've been telling them about for years.

Give thanks in all circumstances; for this
is God's will for you in Christ Jesus.
1 THESSALONIANS 5:18

*I*sn't a new year the perfect time to try some different ideas and make some new resolutions? I would encourage you to try some fresh ways of engaging with your teen: try not to correct as much, learn to laugh, quit lecturing and start having more discussions, stop talking and start listening, and quit complaining and begin seeking a new gratefulness for the opportunities that God has placed in your life.

Your teen wants to be connected to you, and they will openly welcome the changes you make as you strive to parent them with the same kind of discipline, love, and patience that the Lord has demonstrated toward you. Isn't it time for a change?

Brothers and sisters, I do not consider myself
yet to have taken hold of it. But one thing I
do: Forgetting what is behind and straining
toward what is ahead, I press on toward
the goal to win the prize for which God has
called me heavenward in Christ Jesus.

PHILIPPIANS 3:13–14

As you make your New Year's resolutions about dieting, working out, changing habits, and visiting new places, don't forget that you have a wonderful opportunity to make some changes in your relationship with your teen. That could be a vow to develop a deeper relationship, a commitment to listen more and talk less, a guarantee to spend just one more hour a week with your teen, or giving your word to take care of some clutter in your relationship.

Make this the greatest year yet. Don't hold back, and don't save something for that special occasion. That special occasion is today. Take advantage of the remaining time with your teen. Happy New Year, folks! I pray for a great year for you and your family!